Drawing
and Painting
Animals

Drawing
and Painting
Animals

by Fritz Henning

Illustrations by the author except as otherwise identified.

NORTH LIGHT PUBLISHERS
37 Franklin Street • Westport, Connecticut 06881

Published by NORTH LIGHT PUBLISHERS, a division
of FLETCHER ART SERVICES, INC., 37 Franklin
Street, Westport, Conn. 06881.

Distributed to the trade by Van Nostrand Reinhold
Company, 135 West 50th Street, New York, N.Y. 10020.
Manufactured in U.S.A.
First Printing 1981

Library of Congress Cataloging in Publication Data

Henning, Fritz, 1920-
    Drawing and painting animals.

    Bibliography: p.
    Includes index.
    1. Animals in art. 2. Art—Technique. I. Title.
N7660.H46   743'.6   81-3995
ISBN 0-89134-037-4   AACR2
ISBN 0-89134-039-4 (pbk.)

Edited by Carla Dennis
Designed by Fritz Henning
Composition by Stet Shields, Inc.
Color printed by Rose Printing
Printed and bound by The Book Press

For Jane

"Nobody cares how long it takes you to create a
 picture. Nor how tough or easy it was to do,
 and it is of only passing interest *how* you did it.
 In art all that counts is the result. That's
 all anyone will remember."

Albin Henning
(1886-1943)

Albin Henning

Contents

Foreword

It was a long time ago—in fact it's creeping up on fifty years since I first met Harold Von Schmidt. I was a tag-along kid on the long, summertime drive from our home in Pomfret, Connecticut to New York City. My dad was taking a friend, our week-end guest, back to his apartment in Forest Hills. In those dim days before the Merritt Parkway and all the other throughways, the most direct route South after New Haven was down Route 1, the old Boston Post Road. When we reached Westport, for reasons unknown to me, we turned off the highway and wandered around what was then the outskirts of town. After a few misturns and an inquiry at a gas station we found our way to the now familiar white house next to the cemetery on Evergreen Avenue.

We were greeted in the driveway by a sprightly Mr. Von Schmidt, and within a few minutes we all adjourned to the adjacent studio. My dad and Von, I soon discovered, had long been acquainted as both had been students of the mutually revered teacher and painter, Harvey Dunn.

I was used to studios and all the great gear artists collect. My father had a wonderful assortment of army uniforms, helmets, gas masks, old swords and rifles, but nothing had prepared me for Von's vast assemblage. Marvelous stuff was festooned from every nook and cranny. Standing goggle-eyed in a corner, my gaze roamed the big room, taking in everything from the mountain lion skin complete with snarling head, to saddles, boots, buffalo horns, guns, uniforms, hats and all sorts of uniden-tifiable impedimenta. I have no idea how long I stood transfixed. Reality returned when Von took down from a hidden hook a Sioux headdress stream-ing with feathers and solemnly placed it on my head. He then rummaged under some Stetsons and sombreros bringing forth a gunbelt and holster. Bending down, he carefully fastened it around my waist and explained it should be worn high and snug against the body. He then showed me how to draw the pistol. It was a long, heavy Navy Colt, and I could hardly pull it clear of the holster. The operation was something less than a quick draw as both my hands were required to lift and hold the pistol in a shooting position.

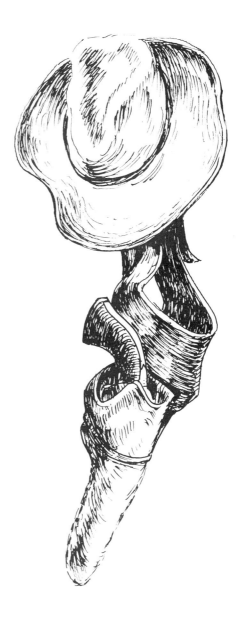

I was eleven years old and I knew that was a day to remember.

I didn't see Von again until 1946, the year I left my seagoing career and came ashore to try to make my way in the world of art. In New York I learned the Society of Illustrators held weekly gatherings for returning veterans which included life drawing classes, critiques and programs of one-on-one sessions with member illustrators at their studios. The latter required signing-up and fixing dates. Von was on the list and I put in my name for an appointment. I was assigned a date to see him about two weeks later.

My portfolio was in sad shape, and I hastened to remedy the situation. The results were dismal in every area. One oil, a group of mounted Arabs charging across the sand dunes, had some verve to it, although the paint quality had as much appeal as yesterday's leftover sandwich. I debated whether or not to include it, but as it was the only picture I had with horses I decided in its favor.

With misgivings I arrived on the appointed hour at Von's studio. It was the same fantastic place I remembered. It looked like nothing had been moved, but more had been added. Von was as gracious as ever, and in due course we came down to the business at hand. I opened my oversized portfolio, revealing the charging Arabs in all their glory. Von looked for a long moment then said in his somewhat squeaky voice: "What are those Arabs doing on Morgans?"

"What?" I stammered, not knowing what he was talking about.

Von immediately retreated to the far corner of the studio and began burrowing behind a cabinet, looking from the rear like a dog about to unearth his favorite bone. And that is what he came up with—bones, all kinds of bones.

"This," he said, holding aloft a large animal skull, "is a Morgan. Notice his Roman nose and the heavy cheek. And here is the skull of an Arabian. Look at his nose...see how dished-in it is and how much thinner..."

With these and other bones as his props Von talked for nearly two hours without a pause. He explained that the Morgan was a native American breed—the only breed ever named after a specific horse: a dark-bay called Justin Morgan. This remarkable stallion lived in the early 1800's in Ver-

mont and sired a string of descendants that passed on to succeeding generations the commendable characteristics that have long made the breed a favored saddle and harness horse. The Morgan was the prize mount of the U.S. Cavalry in its days of glory. A Morgan crossed with an Arabian becomes a Morab, an animal some cowpokes claim to be the best cow horse in the West. I was told about the only thing the Morgan never accomplished was to find his way to the nomads in the North African or Arabian Desert. An Arab would be at home on a camel, a Barb or an Arabian pony. Aboard any other mount he would seem as out of place as if he were wearing a sequined cowboy suit instead of his turban and flowing burnoose.

The light from the studio's big North window was fading when Von drew to a raspy conclusion and I hid the galloping Morgans back in my portfolio. The rest of the pictures had been forgotten. My lesson that day dealt with animal anatomy—a subject worthy of much pursuit.

It was never my intention to specialize exclusively in animal art. I have not done so, but I found my study of animals has brought me an understanding sometimes noticeably lacking in the work of others. It is evident many capable artists who include animals in their pictures never learned the equivalent of my lesson about Arabs riding Morgans.

The key ingredient in learning about animals is *interest*. You have to like animals—all kinds of animals—and study and observe them with more than a passing concentration. Von started me on the way by showing me how to teach myself to think the problem through, to cover all aspects of the subject without getting sidetracked. It is a lesson, along with so many gleaned from my father, I am still trying to digest.

Since my early memorable sessions with Von I have been fortunate to have the opportunity over the years of working closely with him on a frequent basis. These sessions never ceased being revealing and rewarding experiences. Von always gave freely of his time and knowledge, and he has helped many others along the way. All who were lucky enough to have crossed his path are the richer for it.

Fritz Henning
Weston, Connecticut
1980

Introduction

The idea of this book came about on the basis of need. There are a number of excellent publications available on the work of specific artists serving, in the main, as showcases for their interpretations of animals. Few such works, however, deal in more than a cursory way with the basic structure, anatomy, and action patterns of a variety of animals. Nor do they evolve the building of a picture in a logical progression from rough sketch to finished rendering in divers mediums.

Most of the drawings, diagrams and paintings were done specifically to demonstrate points and procedures discussed in the text. The works of many artists, contemporary and otherwise, are included to show a diversity of approach and handling. It should be clearly established in any picture-making procedure, that there is always more than one right way to do it. Indeed, the possible solutions are restricted only by the limitations of the artist.

Writing and putting together a book of this type is a sobering experience. Initial illusions of a happy joyride down ego lane are quickly derailed by the magnitude of the task. Questions abound. It is a time for self-doubt; it is a time for reflection.

Looking back from the vantage point of thirty-odd years in the business of making pictures and trying to teach others to do so, has saddled me with some deep-seated conclusions. One has to do with what it takes "to be an artist"; another deals with the puzzling process of "how we learn."

I'm convinced almost everyone has the capability of being some kind of an artist. We all possess artistic ability—the difference is a matter of degree. Anyone who has observed the visual expressions of young children must realize a fundamental art facility exists in the human animal. The inevitable reduction in proficiency with advancement in age is caused by our questionable schooling priorities often resulting in an unrequited transference of interest. The fact remains, if you have a compelling fascination for creating visual images, along with the stomach and stamina for hard work, you *will* be capable of producing pictures of merit.

Certainly it helps to have a portion of that illusive stuff known as talent. But talent itself is not the determining factor in being an artist. Over the years I have come to know, on a close basis, many scores of artists—people who make their living by creating pictures. I have also observed the works and efforts of thousands of students who hoped to become artists. It is amply apparent many individuals who possess more than their share of native talent fail to make full use of their ability. They lack the interest and drive necessary to produce worthy work. Possibly it is all too easy for them.

On the other hand, many individuals develop into competent professionals who have but a modicum of talent. What they have is a consuming interest and determination to succeed. They make the most of what they have. In the long run their work may fall short of greatness, but the immediate results are rewarding and respectable.

Classroom teachers attest to the fact each student marches to an inner cadence. We all learn at varying speeds and for various reasons. We seem to learn when we want to learn and when we are ready to learn. Parents know this, too. They see one child start to walk at 10 months and his brother will be content to crawl into his 15th month. One child will speak clearly at 18 months; another normal infant will take much longer to talk effectively. And so it is with every phase of learning, no matter what the discipline or how advanced and complicated it may be.

No one really knows how we learn anything. The most logical answer is that we teach ourselves. What we refer to as *teaching* is, at best, creating a suitable environment conducive to self-edification.

So it is with any phase in the study of art. No one can take your hand and show you how to paint a portrait, run a wet-in-wet wash, draw animals or any of the other things that appeal to you unless you are ready to teach yourself. We can discuss art history, the theory of color and the vicissitudes of composition, but no one can show you how to translate the image in your eye and mind to a drawing or painting you want to create. In the moment of truth, it is all up to you. If you have the interest and desire the time will come when you will be able to put it all together. When you do it will be based on the information and help you seek to satisfy your particular needs at the time you need it.

Perhaps time, circumstance and the approach to animal drawing emphasized here will supply the impetus you need to teach yourself what you want and need to know. The degree of skill you achieve will depend on your ability and, more importantly, on your determination. If you have the desire, it is hoped this book will supply the information you need and nudge you on your way.

Observation 1

"The organ of sight is one of the quickest, and takes in at a single glance an infinite variety of forms; notwithstanding, it cannot perfectly comprehend more than one object at a time."

Leonardo da Vinci
(1452-1519)

Few subjects have more universal appeal than animals. Everyone is fascinated by the habits, movement and antics of our warm-blooded fellow inhabitants of Earth. Every culture and every period, from Stone Age cave wall drawings to the exhibits of contemporary artists in today's glass galleries bear witness to the inspiration animals offer us. Yet, with all this interest and heritage, many otherwise competent artists shy away from drawing and painting animals. They feel animal forms and actions are too complex to comprehend, and they leave the subject to the specialist. This is a shame.

Animals are not that difficult to draw, and it shouldn't take years of special study to feel sufficiently secure to include them in your pictures. Like most drawing and learning, the clue is observation and applying to the subject information you already know. And you'll be surprised at the extent of your present animal knowledge. Let's consider some of the things you know but may not realize you know about animals.

Although you're probably not familiar with the proper anatomical names of all the bones and muscles of your body, you are likely to have a pretty good idea of where they are, how they move and function. Much of this information can be applied directly to any animal, even birds! Except for the clavicles (collar bones) which we have in common only with the ape family, the human skeleton and muscle pattern is remarkably similar to the dog, horse, cow, cat, deer, elephant and all other creatures great and small.

The relationship of our head, for instance, to that of the horse is an easy association. Similarly, the spine, rib cage and other major parts probably aren't hard to visualize. However, it gets a little more difficult to understand structural similarity when it comes to the hands and feet. In this area here is the thing to remember: Our fingernails and

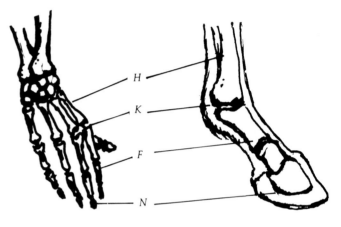

H	Hand	N	Nails
K	Knuckle	T	Thumb
F	Fingers		

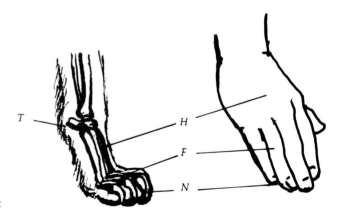

The hand compared to the foreleg of the horse and cat.
These diagrams are not in size relationship.

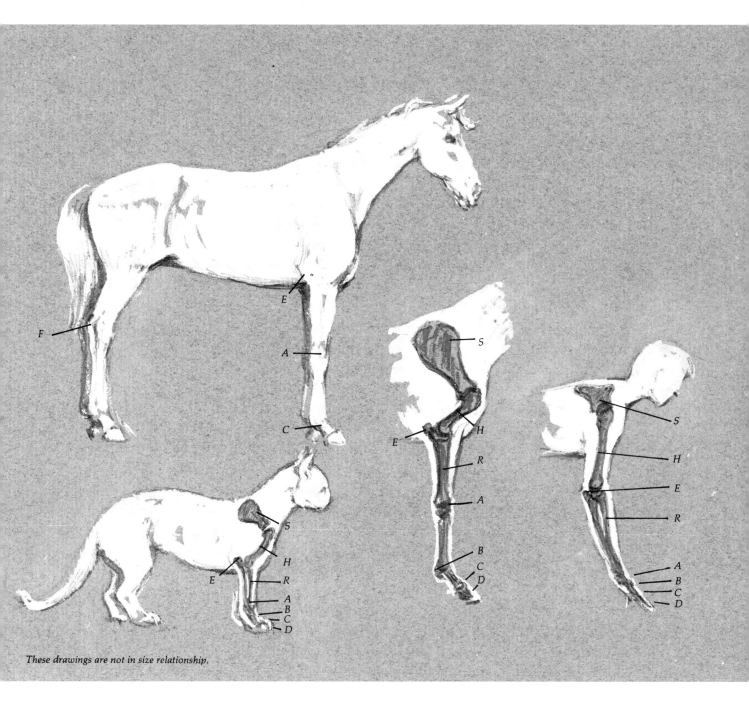

These drawings are not in size relationship.

The arm and shoulder compared to the horse and cat.

A   Wrist (On a horse it is called the knee)

B   Knuckle

C   Fingers (Called pastern on a horse)

D   Nails (Claws on a cat; hoof on a horse)

E   Elbow

F   Ankle (It is called the hock of a horse. Note it is always higher than the knee, or properly wrist, of the foreleg.)

H   Upper arm (humerus)

R   Lower arm (radius-ulna)

S   Shoulder (In humans the shoulder forms are held apart by the collar bones. Horses, dogs, cats, etc. do not have clavicles.)

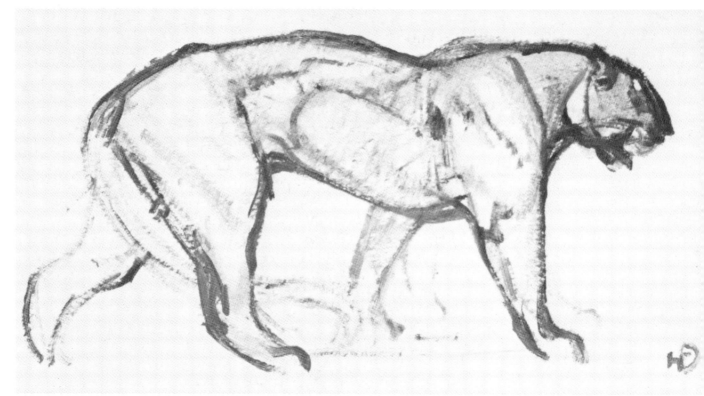

Henri Deluermoz
Tiger, Brush and ink

an animal's hoofs or paws are basically the same. For example, in the horse the bones of the fingers (phalanx) are grouped together in an area called the pastern, the end of which is attached to the hoof. In short, the horse stands on the equivalent of our fingernails. These are lumped together as one large unit rather than five separate small ones. Have a close look at the diagram comparing the relationship of the hand to the corresponding animal structures. Once you grasp the relationship of the human hand to the horse's foot or the cat's paw, the rest is easy. You'll readily understand that the difference between species is mainly one of proportions and surface covering. Equipped with this knowledge you can apply most of what you know about drawing the figure to drawing animals.

The next phase of learning to draw animals is likely to require a little research. You should know certain basics about the animals you want to draw so that you can better understand their peculiar proportions. As an example, let's consider the cat. What do you know about cats?

You know they have a head, four legs, a tail, fur and whiskers. And, of course, you now know all about their paws and how they relate to the human hand. All of this information is good, but it's not enough for an artist.

To capture the feeling and personality of a cat we must know its physical characteristics plus something of its habits and purpose in being. We know, for instance, the cat is carnivorous and, if wild, would live by catching other animals. Unlike dogs that hunt mainly by a sense of smell, the cat is a "sight" hunter. He relies on keen vision, stealth and surprise attack. The cat moves with grace, power and silence. He has a long, cylindrical body and a short rib cage in relation to the length of his spine. This allows for great body flexibility. Close observation will show the cat's skull is wider than any other part of his body. If a cat can get his head through an opening he knows he can pull the rest of his body through. In this regard his whiskers become more than facial decoration: they act as "feelers" and let him know if the hole is going to be a tight squeeze or one that can be negotiated with abandon.

The crouch is the cat's natural stance. The hind legs are longer than the front, enabling the animal to spring and jump with much power. The walking stride, like that of many animals, is timed so the

Leonardo da Vinci

back foot lands exactly where the corresponding front foot was. He has great patience and can remain motionless for long periods. A cat on the hunt always appears relaxed, at ease, and in control.

With a little study similar information can be found about other animals that interest you. Mountains of research material is available at most libraries on anything from dogs to reptiles. And zoos offer a fine opportunity for first hand observation and direct sketching of animal types not otherwise available.

The next step is to take all your new found knowledge and start drawing. How to begin? You know a lot of facts now, but how do you use them? As with all drawing, first you have to get to the basics and *simplify*.

Unfortunately, Leonardo did not map out for us the equivalent of a basic figure for animals, although we can thank him for a number of notes on the proportions of the horse. However, with a little ingenuity and adjustment in proportions we can adapt the principles of basic figure drawing to serve us well in drawing animals. With a little practice you should be able to maneuver these simplified forms to construct any kind of animal you have researched.

There is one more major problem to ponder before you can put it all together and include animals in your repertoire of paintable subjects. That is action.

Animals move with a precise leg sequence. This pattern should be learned, understood and *felt* if you hope to achieve believable drawings. Because we walk upright on two legs it is difficult to relate to locomotion on four feet. It is true we naturally swing our arms in a reciprocal rhythm with the movement of our legs as we walk or run. In general, this corresponds with the basic action of most animals. This similarity becomes obscure in analyzing the gallop, and has no bearing at all on the pace or leap.

Like people, animals can and do assume a wide variety of actions. Photographs of bucking horses or bulls demonstrate incredible contortions. Such actions, however, are fleeting and do not constitute a normal, logical motion. To illustrate a convincing animal under usual conditions the action you choose must be typical. Few things are more visually disturbing than an animal ambulating with an incorrect stride. Even the untrained observer will sense something is wrong and out of balance. There is no doubt you'll need some knowledge of action and foot sequence if you want to include in your picture an animal doing more than standing at attention.

Although many species have peculiarities in style of movement, most animal action can be reduced to these basic gaits: *walk, trot, pace* (sometimes called *rack*), *gallop* and *leap*.

In subsequent chapters we will examine and discuss five categories of animals. This will include an analysis of the normal movement patterns of each group as well as their basic construction, proportions and dominant characteristics. The emphasis will be on familiar, domesticated types, namely the dog, horse, cat and bovine families. The fifth group will deal with what we'll call *special* animals, i.e., the bear, giraffe, elephant and others with unusual proportions and singular qualities. There will also be a section covering some of the characteristics of birds.

Before we get down to cases about drawing animals, there are a few general considerations to cover. These have to do with the unique problems of observing and studying animals.

As with all drawing, it is wise to bring to your subject as much knowledge as you can. You may not use all the research you collect, but the knowledge you gain is never wasted. Drawing directly from animals can be a great help and is recommended. Perforce most of your direct observation drawings will be quick sketches—very quick in most cases. From our friendly household pets to caged beasts in a zoo, animals are almost constantly in motion—particularly when you start to draw them. Even when asleep they move. Unless anesthetized, or holding a rigid trained stance, you will seldom have more than a few seconds to capture the form, action, mood and details you want. Photographs and other reference material are essential and can be a great help. You will soon discover, however, they also present a danger.

Copying photographs too closely may result in a loss of the essence of the animal—often the real reason for wanting to create the drawing. Also, heavy reliance on specific reference is likely to lead to static, sterile and unsympathetic interpretations. Reference material is often necessary, but use it wisely—don't let it use you. Capturing the *spirit* of the subject is more important than cataloging the facts, no matter how accurately they are recorded. To assure drawing quality requires training your

---

On the opposite page are two examples of man's early approaches to drawing animals. The top picture is a pencil rendering based on a cave wall painting of a bison said to have been done 25,000 years ago. Our Stone Age ancestors' ability to graphically describe what was important in their world was profound. As demonstrated here, the bold, simple lines and feeling of bulk capture the essence of the animal to a degree many sophisticated artists would like to emulate. Strangely, primitive artists who displayed such singular skill in interpreting animals left no evidence of comparable facility in recording humans.

The second picture is a drawing from the tomb of Menofre. Art in ancient Egypt took on a rigid, stylized form. Drawings of figures and animals were reduced to flat outlines to express a symbolic meaning. Realism and depth were not considerations. Drawings of people and animals invariably described the head and feet in a profile position, while the eyes are shown as if in a frontal view. The message was intellectual, almost as abstract in meaning as the hieroglyphics shown in the background.

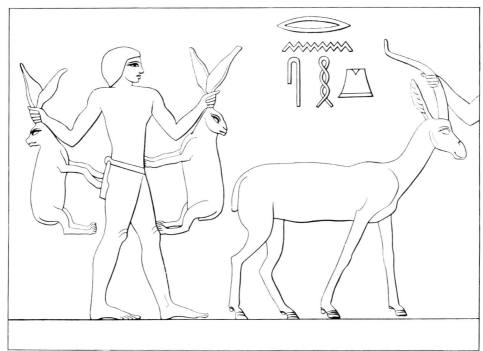

powers of observation so you can remember in your mind's eye the movement, grace and character of the animals you have seen.

For the artist, observation is more than just looking. It is *seeing*, *remembering* and *understanding*. It is the training of the eye as well as the mind to recall the things you've seen at other times under different circumstances. It is not easy to do, and it is a never-ending study, but it can be learned if you want to do it.

A good deal of study has been done in recent years relating to the mysterious ways of the human mind. Our brain, the ultimate in complex computers, is compartmentalized with different sections controlling different functions. It is well-established one part of the brain controls what can be roughly called our feeling actions, while another section deals with more precise reasoning. For example, when concentrating on adding a column of numbers, or even approximating the measurement of a horse's leg in relation to the depth of his body, we would be using that portion of our brain that deals with exact and concrete matters. On the other hand, if we listen to music or enjoy a pastoral scene, the feeling section of the brain would be in control.

A case can be made that such knowledge should be applied to the act of drawing. Logic suggests that by concentrating on precise proportions, scale, measurements, as well as manual dexterity, we are utilizing that portion of the mind not best suited to the ultimate purpose of drawing. If, in drawing, we concentrate on *looking* and avoid as much as possi-

The action of any animal can be established best with quick, rough sketches such as this. Work in any medium you like and try to suggest the flow and rhythm throughout the body. Think only about the action—don't be concerned, at this point, with details, texture or refinements of rendering. Plenty of time for that later.

ble the exact aspects of the forms in front of us we will be better able to translate what we *see* and *feel*.

There is likely to be considerable truth in this premise. Kimon Nicolaides seemed to be starting down this road a half century ago when he emphasized gesture and contour drawing in his book *The Natural Way to Draw.*

Stated simplistically, the idea is to approach drawing more through *looking* than through the manual skill of scribing lines. It is a hard thing to do. You have to train your hand to follow the dictates of your eye. And, as much as possible, you should do so without constant guidance. To *look* only at your subject and not at what you are drawing is a difficult exercise. Try it. The more you practice the better at it you will become.

I do not believe this procedure, as helpful as it may be, will open the doors to a new world of enlightenment about drawing. However, it may be of help, particularly if it encourages you to record without question what you observe. It takes courage to put down exactly what you see. Many times

Honoré Daumier
Don Quixote

Collection of Claude Roger Marz, Paris

The 19th century French artist, Honoré Daumier was particularly adept at establishing action, gesture and feeling of form with a few loose but meaningful lines. This drawing of Don Quixote is a fine example.

Christian Rohlfs
Amazon, 1912

Folkwang Museum, Essen

An exponent of German Expressionism, Christian Rohlfs was able to achieve a powerful feeling of motion in quite a different way in his painting of the running animals.

Heinrich Kley
A remarkably clever artist and satirist, Kley drew animals doing unbelievable things in a most believable way. He had a superb knowledge of animal anatomy and action that allowed him to make the outlandish appear plausible.

a pose, action, or effect of color will appear so unreal or distorted you tend to compromise and say this cannot be, and alter what you observe to something intellectually safe. Unfortunately, the result is also likely to be unexciting and less than a truthful statement.

The biggest thing you have going for you in drawing animals is that you like them. I have never heard of an artist who was any good at drawing animals who did not have a high regard and respect for their special talents and individuality. The first step, then, in learning to draw animals is to like them. With this impetus you will observe and study with an interest and intensity you could not bring to subjects you consider more prosaic. If your attitude about animals in general is ho-hum and as stimulating as a Payne's gray day, you might as well forget about learning to draw them. If, on the other hand, you really like them, there is no reason you cannot learn to draw them convincingly.

The American artist Robert Henri enjoyed a remarkable reputation as a teacher. One method he employed to help train his students in observation was to pose a model in one room and make the students work in another.* The students would observe the model and then return to their easels in the adjacent studio to paint from memory. When memory failed they would trek back for another look at the model. Rumor had it that the corridors between the rooms were a traffic jam. Henri's procedure was similar, but simpler than drawing animals. At least the students in Henri's class would have been reasonably sure the model was in the same position when they returned to recycle their observation. With an animal you can bet every time you look you will encounter a different pose.

Direct drawing, trained memory observation, the judicial use of reference material and study are the ingredients you need to make the most of your talents and interest in drawing and painting animals. Of all these, *interest* is the most important. Without interest it is unlikely you would have read this far...since you have, let's go on and dig into the details of drawing animals that will make it all worthwhile.

The text of this book follows a logical sequence with as little redundancy as possible. Even though your main interest may be to concentrate on one or two types of animals, it is recommended you study all chapters in order. Frequently details mentioned in one section may not be as fully covered in another. Obviously, many points of observation, drawing and rendering are applicable to all animals, and some bit of information you discover about a dog or cat may prove useful in drawing a horse.

---

*Evidence suggests Henri learned this procedure from his teacher, Thomas Eakins. However, the author first heard the story from Stuart Davis, the noted abstract painter, who had been a student of Henri.

Drawing

"We fail to express things as they are,
as they really are, without remembering
having looked at them."

Gertrude Stein (1874-1946)

According to Michelangelo, "Drawing is the fountainhead and substance of painting, sculpture, architecture, and the root of all sciences." Nowadays the "all sciences" part of his statement seems mildly overblown, but few artists past or present will quarrel with the rest of the master's premise. Assuredly, the lack of knowledge and some skill in drawing precludes the creation of believable, representational pictures. Drawing as such, however, need not be thought of as an exquisite, seemingly spontaneous rendering that oozes from a master's hand like readi-mix frosting from a pastry tube. Even for the genius the virtuoso performance takes years of study and concentrated practice. There is no mystique to drawing; anyone with the desire can acquire a fair degree of proficiency. Drawing can be compared to playing a musical instrument—with but a drop of dexterity most people can achieve reasonable control. Few of us will make it to the league of Heifetz or Horowitz, but we will be able to play a tune and express ourselves with some personal satisfaction.

In a broad sense, drawing is a *search.* It is the artist's means to discover the line, form, structure, placement and values that will make the particular subject meaningful. The process of drawing helps us translate observed reality with all its variety to the flat, two-dimensional surface on which we strive to project a three-dimensional image. To draw well is no mean accomplishment.

Unfortunately, there is no known method that can make learning to draw effortless. One thing is certain—you can't learn to draw by just reading about it. It takes study, observation and practice. Given these ingredients and the will to succeed, you'll be surprised at the progress you can make, even if you start with the silly cliché assumption you can't draw a straight line.

One thing that often discourages the novice is the apparent ease and rapidity with which the more experienced artist arrives at a final drawing. He seemingly skips a number of the steps the floundering beginner must struggle through. Such shorthand comes about through practice. In time you learn to do some of the drawing steps mentally, without actually putting them on paper. It's like learning the alphabet so you don't have to recite *a* to *m* to know where *n* is. Until you thoroughly learn all the steps in making a drawing and understand their importance, it is best not to skip any. In time you'll discover your own shortcuts.

The steps necessary in drawing an animal are basically the same for drawing the figure, but a little more difficult because your model won't stand still. Also, you probably haven't spent your life studying animals the way you have your fellow humans.

The first phase is to capture the spirit of the pose or action. Generally this is referred to as a *gesture* drawing. It should be a loose, free, rapid sketch to

Heinrich Kley

Eugene Delacroix

Louvre, Paris

25

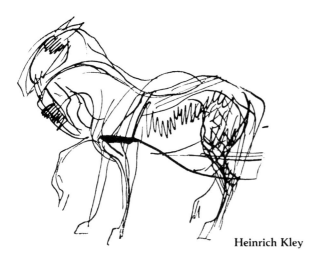

Heinrich Kley

suggest the feeling of the forms and the lines of movement rather than any specific details. Usually the essence of the action or pose can be done in a few moments. If one sketch doesn't work, try another. It is not worthwhile to work over them.

The next step is to try to understand the form and dimension of what you are drawing. This should grow out of the action you established in the gesture drawing. Work boldly at the early stages. Don't tighten up or worry about details—time enough for that later. Remember your drawing at this stage is not for exhibition, you are not doing it for anyone to look at and admire. The only purpose is to search and probe so you can understand the form, build structure and control the action of the animal. Work in any medium you like and at any size you find comfortable. Most people find pencil or charcoal most suitable.

With a little study, animals can be reduced to a relatively few simple basic forms. In most cases the forms can be based on a modified cylinder. It is helpful at the beginning to "draw through" to fix in your mind the form's solid, three-dimensional quality. The manner I have illustrated the basic forms is arbitrary. It works for me, it may be helpful to you. If, however, you find other ways that are more meaningful to you by all means use them. There are no absolutes to worry about in drawing. Any way it works for you is fine.

Some artists who gain sufficient experience are often able to skip many details of the form drawing and proceed directly to the refinements. Robert Fawcett, a superb draughtsman, used to deride teaching students to "draw through." He would storm, "I don't give a damn about all those stove

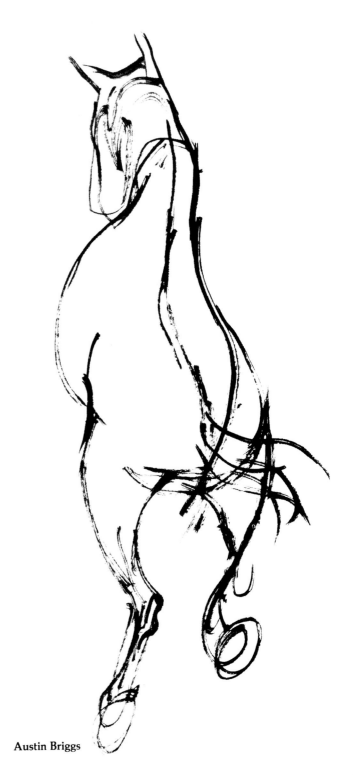

Austin Briggs

Henri de Toulouse-Lautrec

pipes. What interests me is what I see—the surface." This was fine for Bob as he had an extremely
accurate eye and years of study and drawing experience to support him. I wouldn't advise any beginner
to try to jump ahead too quickly. In time you'll
drop some of the preliminary procedure naturally.
When you really understand the forms you will automatically skip unnecessary stages because you are
sure of what you are about, and your mind will
race ahead of your hand.

Somewhere in the process of building the forms
you should begin to think about where the light is
coming from and how strongly it should be represented to create the kind of effect you want. Decisions, decisions...creating a picture is full of them.

After the gesture, form, light and shadow, and
value pattern are worked out and settled to your
satisfaction, you can say your preliminary drawing
is done and you can proceed to a finished rendering

if you so desire. We will discuss different mediums
and how to handle them as we go along. Remember, however, no matter what medium you use for
your final rendering, you should still *draw*. Drawing doesn't stop when you pick up a brush or start
working with some tool other than the one you
normally consider your drawing instrument. Not to
think in terms of drawing when you render will
likely result in a diminished *feeling* of the action
and less solidity of the form.

The general procedure of establishing a drawing
as outlined here will be incorporated in each of the
specific animal types we take up in detail. Repeti-
tion is one of the cornerstones of learning, and this
approach should help you to improve your ability
to draw. There is little doubt good drawing is the
basis of good pictures. And there is no doubt some
ability to draw can be acquired with study and
practice, practice, practice.

Drawing what you see—and don't see

The phenomena of photography and all its kindred marvels of television with stop action, slow motion, instant replays and the like have become such a part of our visual experience most of us accept it as reality. It is not. The artist in particular should keep in mind we do not see things the way the camera records them. Under usual circumstances the closest we come to *seeing* what a photograph reveals is when we compare a static, immobile scene to the camera's product of the same scene, taken at the same point of observation under the same lighting conditions. Even then it is not likely the lens of the camera and those in our eyes will have a similar focal range. Also, the color in the developed photo will be but a chemical approximation of the spectrum we see. It may be pleasing, but it is not accurate. In truth, our vision and the world about us as recorded by the camera have little in common.

Never is this more apparent than when we at-tempt to analyze what we see in a fast-moving ac-tion such as a running or jumping animal. What we see is a blur. On the other hand, high speed photo-graphs can freeze almost any action, allowing us to study something we can't see. As indicated earlier, such photographic information can be helpful to the artist if used wisely, but to copy what the camera sees as a substitute for our own vision and reactions to the scene is foolishness.

The above photograph has much useful informa-tion. The calf's leg action is expressive, and a little study shows how each leg bends and overlaps the others. There is a nice thrust to the body and neck, and the larger forms of the body are clearly de-fined. Discounting for the moment the merits and de-merits of working from photos, let's consider the photo of the calf as a common point of reference and see how it can be used in drawing. (For this exercise the background has been painted out to eliminate confusion.)

Each sketch was done on a separate sheet of visualizing paper, working in progression, one over the other.

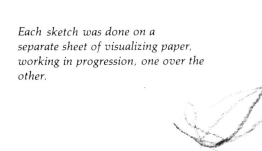

1   The first sketches are to try to create a rough feeling of the action. In gesture drawing keep it simple and spontaneous. Just express the thrust of the movement and don't worry about exact forms or refinements.

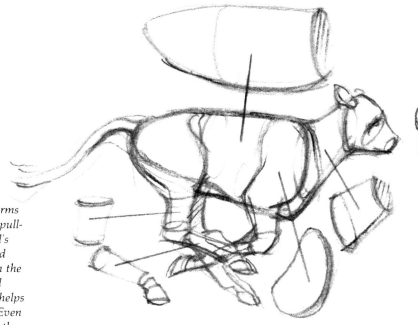

2   The gesture is refined into basic forms to get the feeling of the bulk. The pullouts show how most of the animal's forms can be simplified to modified cylinders. It helps to draw through the forms this way to fix in your mind their solidity and position. It also helps in controlling the foreshortening. Even though this is a straight side view, the legs, in particular, have definite in and out movement as well as the obvious back and forth action.

3   Light and shadow are suggested and the forms further refined and developed. The drawing at this stage can be an end in itself or serve as a basis for a finished rendering.

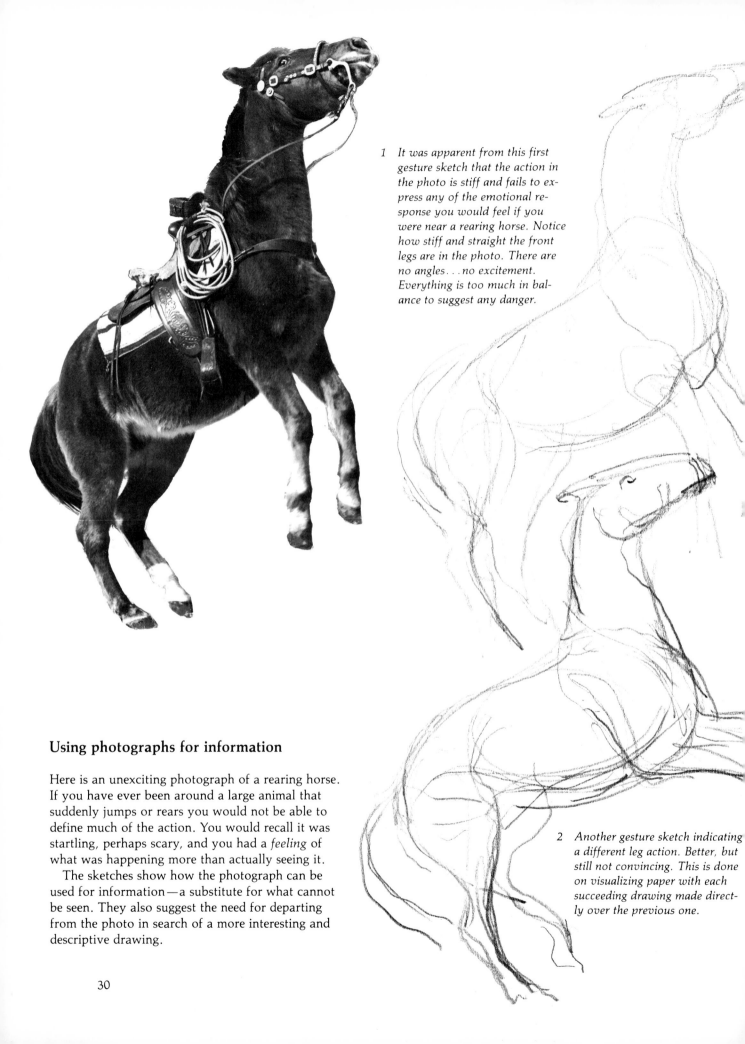

1 It was apparent from this first gesture sketch that the action in the photo is stiff and fails to express any of the emotional response you would feel if you were near a rearing horse. Notice how stiff and straight the front legs are in the photo. There are no angles...no excitement. Everything is too much in balance to suggest any danger.

2 Another gesture sketch indicating a different leg action. Better, but still not convincing. This is done on visualizing paper with each succeeding drawing made directly over the previous one.

Using photographs for information

Here is an unexciting photograph of a rearing horse. If you have ever been around a large animal that suddenly jumps or rears you would not be able to define much of the action. You would recall it was startling, perhaps scary, and you had a *feeling* of what was happening more than actually seeing it.

The sketches show how the photograph can be used for information—a substitute for what cannot be seen. They also suggest the need for departing from the photo in search of a more interesting and descriptive drawing.

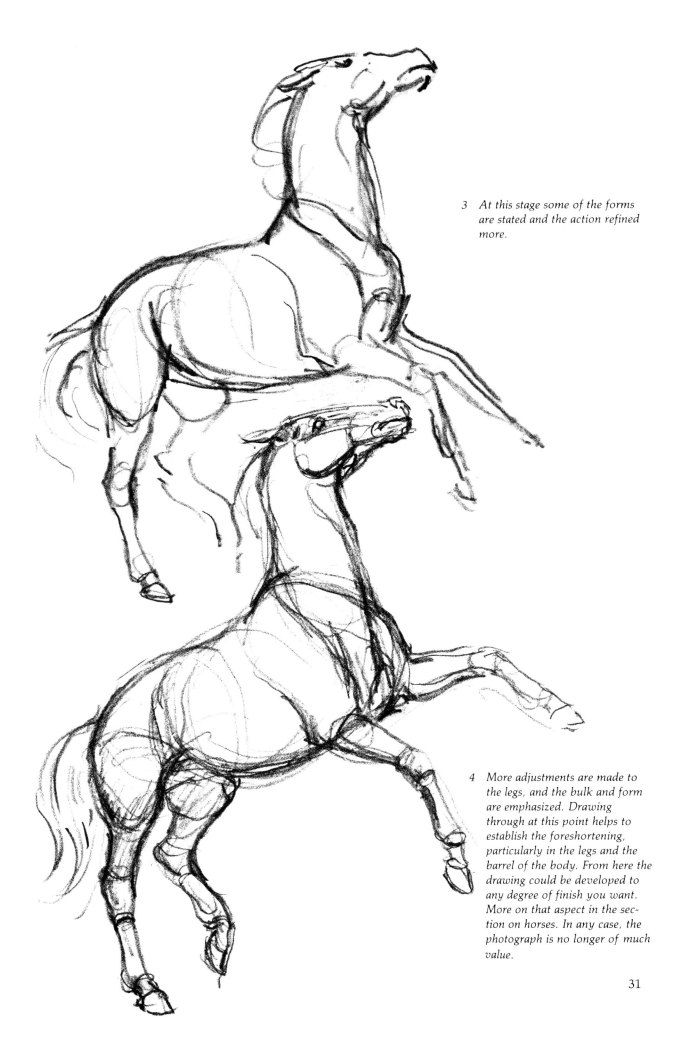

3 At this stage some of the forms are stated and the action refined more.

4 More adjustments are made to the legs, and the bulk and form are emphasized. Drawing through at this point helps to establish the foreshortening, particularly in the legs and the barrel of the body. From here the drawing could be developed to any degree of finish you want. More on that aspect in the section on horses. In any case, the photograph is no longer of much value.

31

Franklin McMahon

Importance of personal response

Franklin McMahon has built a successful career of being an artist/reporter. He believes, and proves his contention, the artist can record a scene in a personal way not possible through photography. The artist's involvement and reaction to an event suggest to the viewer a sense of excitement and presence not often evident in photographs. This sketch of a rodeo bucking horse is an example. How much more exciting and suggestive it is than a static photo such as that of the rearing horse just examined.

As you can see, McMahon is not overly concerned with accuracy or details. He is interested in projecting the noise, smell, action and feeling of the place. It is a quality an artist should always strive to bring to his pictures. It is something he can supply that is seldom seen through mechanical means. Unfortunately, far too many artists are content to simply render a photo as a substitute for a short-changed sense of reality.

Dogs 3

"That which is commonplace will always
be the greatest thing in art."

Harvey Dunn (1884-1952)

Few will argue the old saw that dog is man's best friend. A part of our heritage, prominently noted in every age and culture, dogs flourish in any environment. They are at home and useful in all corners of the world from the white wastes of the arctic to the tropics; from the desert to the farm, and they are found in abundance in the towering cliffs of our modern cities. Depending on the mood of the moment dogs are beautiful, ugly, lovable, mean, smart, stupid, brave, cowardly, eager, lazy, useful or useless. We extol them, pamper, spoil, kick or curse them. One thing is certain, we don't do without them.

Dogs are a part of our lives, our literature, our language. Who has not referred to: a *dog's* life . . . *dog* in the manger . . . in the *dog*house . . . mad *dog* . . . *dog* tired? We let "sleeping *dogs* lie," and "bark up the wrong tree." We know "the tail can wag the *dog*" and we hope "barking *dogs* won't bite." Poets proclaimed, "Every *dog* will have his day"; and navigators for thousands of years have observed Sirius, the *dog* star, and the brightest in the heavens, follow Orion the hunter on his endless course across the sky.

It is hard to imagine a time when man and his faithful, four-legged companion did not co-exist and share the work, trials and joys of living. Apparently there was such a time, but it was more than 15 million years ago. Scientific evidence indicates the dog has romped the earth for at least that long. The forerunner of all Canis familiaris is said to be a creature called the Tomarctus. This small, civet-like animal was the common ancestor of the four major groups of wild dogs from which developed the 100-plus domesticated breeds recognized today. Tomarctus and his four offshoots are all extinct, but their descendants live on and, in one way or another, affect each of us.

With the canine world so much a part of our lives, it is small wonder pictures of dogs are among the most popular of subjects. Nearly every artist responds to their presence. Like our Stone Age forebears who tamed and trained them and left their images on cave walls, bone carvings and artifacts, we feel the need to record our omnipresent friend.

Drawing dogs requires a special kind of patience. Next to the cat they are our most available models and, without a doubt, our worst. They seem to move all the time. Even if you feel you are thoroughly familiar with your subject it is advisable to do some careful research about the particular breed or type of dog you want to draw. Dogs probably vary in proportion, purpose and special characteristics more than any other animal. The range in size is phenomenal. The ShihTzu, for example, weighs but a few pounds and stands only about nine inches at the withers when fully grown; at the other end of the telescope, the Irish Wolfhound and Great Dane can extend over six feet when standing on their hind legs, and weigh upwards to 150 pounds. Most strange features of dogs have been bred into them by special design. The snubnosed bulldog is a fine

Dogs make poor models as they are almost constantly in motion. Quick sketches help. Try to capture the essence of the action. Considering the basic forms makes it easier to control the foreshortening.

35

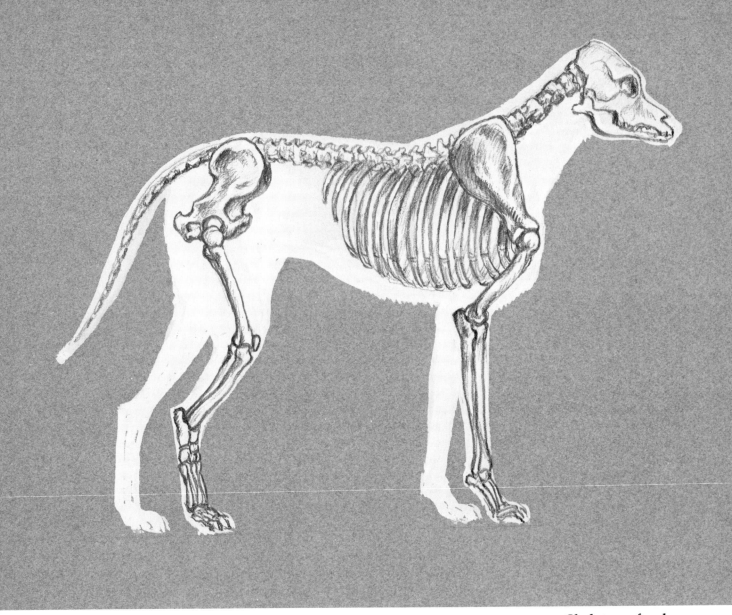

Skeleton of a dog

example. This little fellow was trained to fight and control bulls by clamping his teeth on the bull's neck. The shape of the dog's snout allowed him to breathe as he held on tenaciously to his powerful adversary. This extreme David and Goliath match-up usually worked because there was no way the bull could free himself from his tiny tormentor. In his confusion and frustration the giant bovine became a more manageable beast.

Have you ever wondered why some dogs have all that hair over or around their eyes? It is not for looks or to improve their vision. In breeds such as Scottish terriers who were hunters trained to burrow underground for their quarry, the overgrown brows help to keep the dirt out of their eyes. Also, the unusual proportions of the Dachshund are attributed to the special physical requirements of tunneling for game. The short, strong legs and long, narrow body are better suited to the chase underground than on the surface. Except for the unfortunate tendency of some breeders in recent times to develop purebreds to achieve an idealized show appearance at the sacrifice of intelligence, stamina and purpose, most dogs have been bred to allow them to perform their natural work function more ably. If you search sufficiently you'll usually find a logical explanation for any of the puzzling canine characteristics.

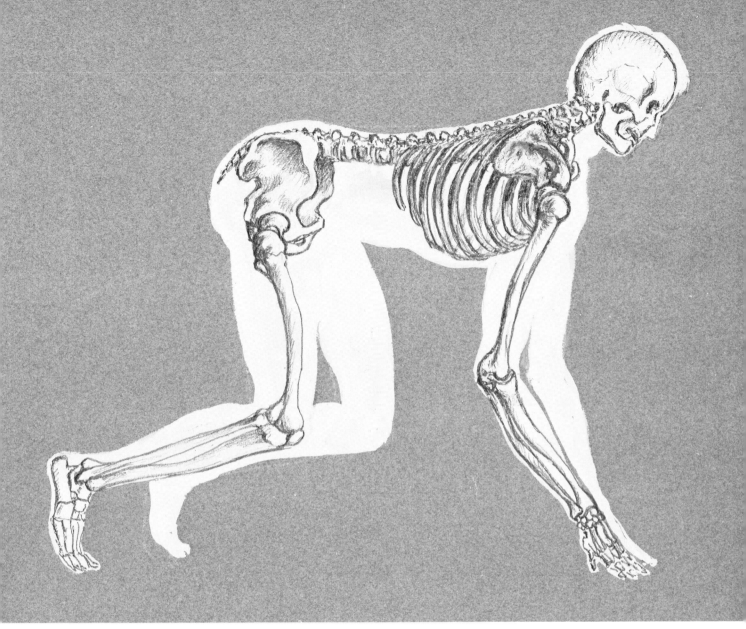

Skeleton of a man

A careful comparison of the human skeleton to that of
a dog will help you better understand the animal's construction and action. As pointed out earlier, it is wise
to apply what you know about human anatomy and
drawing the figure to drawing animals. With a man
posed supported on his fingers and toes as most animals stand, it is easy to see the similarities and the differences in the basic structure.

In relation to the length of the arms and legs, man
has a short body compared to that of the dog. Notice
how much shorter the dog's hind legs are in relation to
the human legs. Also, man's shoulders are held out
from the body by the collar bones, whereas dogs, like
most animals, have no clavicles and the shoulder
draws in closely to the rib cage. (Refer to x-ray on the
following page).

These diagrams are not meant to indicate exact size
relationship, but they are close if you consider the dog
to be a large breed. Although the size and proportions
of dogs vary greatly, there is no basic skeletal difference between large and small dogs.

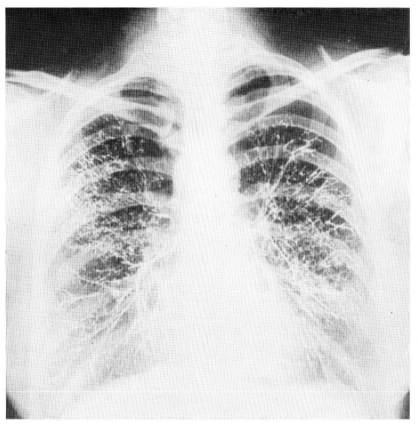

This X-ray of a human chest clearly shows the position and function of the clavicles (collarbones). They are connected to the tip of the shoulder above the ball joint of the upper arm, and to the breast bone. This holds the shoulders, and consequently the arms, out away from the rib cage. The basic structural difference between man and animals (except members of the ape family) is that the animals do not have clavicles; as a result their shoulders ride down alongside the ribs.

Books abound on dogs. Specialized magazines are full of information about the exploits of specific breeds. Any library has a wealth of material from general encyclopedic data to esoteric essays and ponderous scientific journals. All can be helpful and give you an insight into the characteristics of any type dog that interests you. Equipped with even a minimal knowledge of this sort, plus photographs and other reference material, you will be ready to support your direct observation sufficiently to assure reasonable success in drawing your favorite pooch.

When starting to draw dogs be sure to apply what knowledge you have of the human figure. The proportions, of course, are vastly different, but the breakdown of the basic forms is rather similar. Also, it is best to follow the procedure you would in drawing the figure.

First try to capture the basic gesture of the pose and action. As Nicolaides put it, "Draw not what the thing looks like, not even what it is, but what it is DOING." Then start to build up the form and structure without losing the essence of the pose, gesture and action. It's at this stage you should establish the proportions and bring the foreshortening under control. Don't worry about the surface details and texture until you have solved the structure problems. Texture and details are but the frosting on the cake; they must come last, after the ingredients are properly proportioned, mixed and baked. Only then will the frosting fulfill its job.

By this time your model has probably shifted into at least six different positions if, indeed, he hasn't taken off to perform more important duties like chasing the cat or protecting the homestead from the incursion of the deliveryman. You must either wait until you can coax the rascal back, hopefully to assume a somewhat similar position or, if you are determined to carry on, the time has come to rely on inspiration and your memory of earlier observations, supported by whatever material you have in your research files. Along about this juncture I find a saying of Harvey Dunn wise and appropriate: "Don't be so concerned with facts that you can't see beyond them. Things [pictures] too often stop with the fact when actually they should begin there."

Assuming you have the patience and stamina to continue, the next phase of your drawing should be to consider the source and direction of the lighting. Keep it simple and direct to show the form and create interesting patterns of light and dark. Don't forget the end result of an animal picture is no different than a landscape, still life, portrait or an abstraction. The ultimate goal is an interesting relationship of line, value, shape and color. The overall problem is simplified somewhat in the rendering of a single animal, but the broad picture considerations should never be out of mind.

If you wish to complete your preliminary explorations and drawings in another medium, simply proceed in the same manner you would if you were rendering any other subject. The techniques you use in painting animals are no different than those you use in creating a figure, still life, landscape or a flower. As you can see from the examples shown, there is no one way to approach the subject. Do it your own way in any medium you like.

Albrecht Dürer

The renowned German artist drew this Greyhound about 500 years ago. Notice how simply but positively the basic forms of the animal's body are shown. Here are the basic forms of Dürer's dog as I see them.

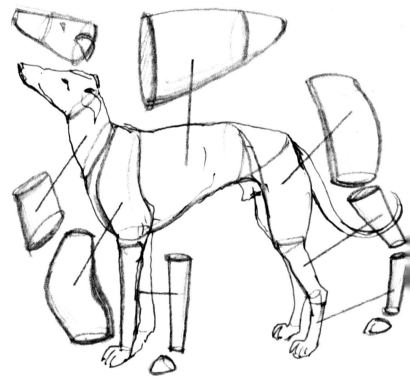

It helps to think of the shoulder and hip muscles as large forms that wrap around and over the barrel of the body. The legs and neck are modified cylinders. Heads vary greatly depending on the breed, but in most cases you can start with an elongated cylinder.

Drawing a dog

1

2

3

4

The best way to draw a dog in a specific action is to study references such as the leg sequence diagrams on opposite page and select an appropriate action. Then roughly indicate the desired movement in a quick gesture sketch as shown in step 1 at the left.

Next, search out the line rhythms that flow through the body. This will help establish the grace and flow of the action. In step 2, notice the line running from the head across the body down through the right hind leg. There is also a nice line going from the outstretched front leg through the body to the tail. At this stage, map out the basic forms of the body to help you work out the significant areas of foreshortening.

In step 3 you start to refine the details and action. Careful observation will show that the weight-bearing legs of the dog do not come straight down from the shoulder to the ground, but they cant inward under the body. Also, as the front legs move forward they are pulled inward as they are lifted; while the hind legs slide inward as they push off, but tend to move outward as they are brought forward. Suggesting this in and out movement, coupled with the simultaneous back and forth action makes for a more believable feeling of motion.

Step 4 requires thought about the lighting and creating a convincing surface pattern. Simplification is called for, but as you begin to render the surface do not lose the feeling of action, form and foreshortening already developed.

Walk

The dog, like most animals, can and does assume a great variety of leg positions in any action. However, there is a definite leg sequence in all of their gaits—walk, trot and gallop. The diagrams shown on page 41 relate to the pattern of leg positions in the continuous movement that constitutes a dog's walk. All dogs, large or small, follow the same sequence.

In the walk the dog usually has three feet on the ground at a time. Some positions such as 2, 3, 6 and 7 show instances where the weight is carried by just two legs; however, in positions 3 and 7, one of the non-supporting legs is just about to touch the ground. At the instant of maximum reach, as shown in 2 and 6, the two legs supporting the weight are on opposite sides of the body.

The diagrams from 1 to 8 are an arbitrary selection of leg positions comprising a single stride sequence; (after 8 the sequence returns to position 1, etc.). When illustrating a dog walking there are many identifiable in-between positions you could select, but remember, the movement relationship of each of the legs should remain consistent with the pattern shown.

1

2

3

4

5

6

7

8

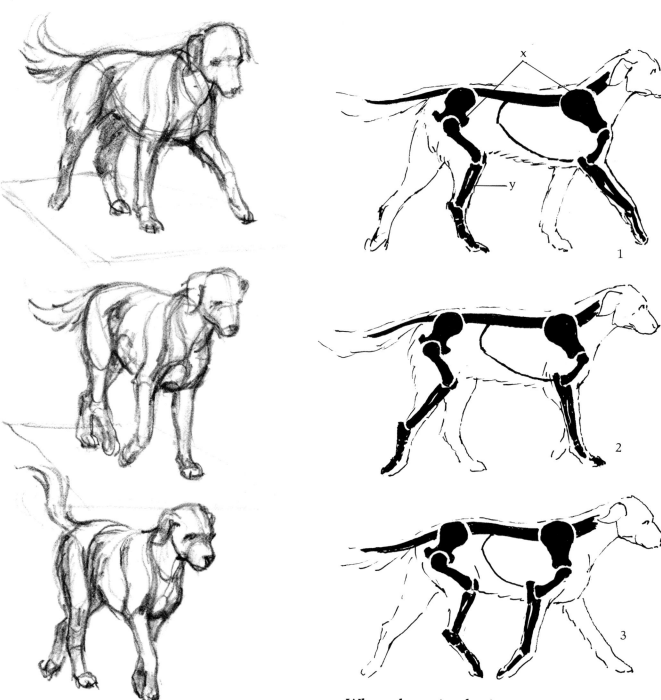

Foreshortened view

When drawing a walking action in other than a straight side view, you may find it helpful to approach the problem this way: First, work out a rough gesture diagram of the pose you want based on one of the definite leg positions as illustrated on page 41. Next, consider the perspective of the ground plane and begin to build up the basic forms of the animal in the desired position. Keep in mind the flowing line rhythms and adjust the foreshortening as necessary so it looks correct. There is no formula to accomplish this. You must base your decisions on your own observation and be content with what appears right to your eye.

Where the action begins

In drawing any animal in action, keep in mind where the motion begins. The key pivot points are in the shoulders and the hip joints (x). In these simplified skeletal diagrams study the way the bones move in a trotting action. This movement directly affects the position of the large forms you see on the surface.

In the hind legs compare how the tibia and fibula (y), in the illustrated positions have measurably different lengths. In diagram 1 the right hind leg is bearing weight, and in this position slants inward under the dog's body, making foreshortening neces-

1

2

3

4

5

6

sary. In diagram 2 less foreshortening is required as the paw lifts off the ground. While in 3 greater foreshortening is apparent as the leg is canted inward under the body so it will clear the ground as it moves forward.

Such in and out movement causing foreshortening is evident in all animal leg action.

Trot *(Refer to sketches above)*

The trot is a kind of speeded-up walk. In the acceleration, however, a different foot sequence pattern emerges. In a trot the animal always lifts and moves his legs diagonally, i.e., the right front leg moves forward at the same time as the left rear, and the left front and the right rear legs move forward together. Most of the time two legs on opposite sides are on the ground supporting the animal's weight. Twice during a full stride sequence, all four legs are off the ground at once. This is shown in 2 and 5. Even in a slow action the leg sequence is difficult to see. High speed photographs or slow motion movies are essential for accurate study. After step 6 the sequence reverts to 1.

As noted in the comments about the walk, there are a great number of possible leg positions in any stride sequence, but they are marginal adjustments occuring between each of the six steps illustrated.

Foreshortened views of action

Starting with rough gesture sketches, try to capture the movement and the lines that best explain the action. Study the leg sequence diagrams of the gait and select a logical position to illustrate. Be sure to keep the legs in proper relationship with each other.

Directly over the gesture drawing begin to build up the basic structure of the animal. This is the best way to work out the foreshortening. Make adjustments as necessary, but try not to lose the rhythmic flow of line that expresses the action.

1

2

3

4

5

6

Gallop

When a dog moves faster than a trot he goes into a gait called a *round* or *rotary* gallop. At intervals in this gait all four feet are off the ground at once, as shown in position 2. In the gallop, the animal's weight is carried by one leg at a time, each pushing off in rapid sequence. *(See diagram at right)*

As shown, the legs are alternately under the body or reaching out, producing a kind of rocking motion. At the instant the weight is carried by a front leg, the rear of the body is lifted higher than the forequarters. Conversely, when a rear leg bears the weight, the front of the body will be higher. This creates a constant up and down slant to the body that should be considered for a believable drawing of this gait.

The leg sequence can progress either clockwise or counter-clockwise, depending on the individual dog. In a counterclockwise movement, as shown above, the weight-bearing leg will strike the ground in this order: left front, left rear, right rear and right front. In a clockwise action (not illustrated) the sequence would be right front, right rear, left rear, left front. There are, of course, innumerable leg positions between each of the stages illustrated, but they follow the same pattern.

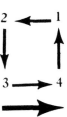

1

2

3

4

Clarence Tillenius

An expert on North American wildlife, this contemporary Canadian illustrator nicely captures the character of wolves following their prey. Notice the positive leg positions clearly indicating the animals' gait — a trot.

Exaggerated action

All animals can progress in a given gait at a variety of speeds. Just as we walk quickly, stroll slowly, jog or run all out, so do animals. With some, mainly the horse, names are ascribed to these special speeds such as the amble, lope, canter, etc. Normally, this kind of refinement is not germane to the action of dogs. However, some of the larger breeds noted for their speed, such as greyhounds and whippets, have an exaggerated gallop that closely resembles a *leap*. This movement deserves a close look.

In a leaping action the hind legs are compressed under the body and spring up and forward in unison as the front legs are lifted together. As all four legs leave the ground they are pulled in under the body, stretch forward and the landing is made with the front feet nearly together. An animal can leap from any gait, but it is usually done from the gallop.

The sequence illustrated on the previous page shows the leap-like motion of the exaggerated gallop.

Leg movement such as this is improbable in small dogs, but cartoonists and illustrators may find it useful to bend reality when they wish to suggest extreme action.

47

Dachshund

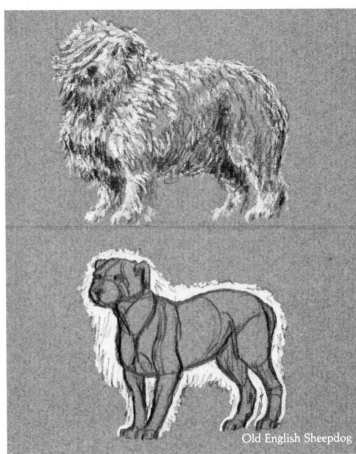

Old English Sheepdog

A dog is a dog, is a dog...

There are so many kinds and types of dogs it is easy to become confused. Probably the most troublesome areas are the proportions and surface coverings. The animal's characteristics are fairly discernible on a large, short-haired dog such as a pointer or a Great Dane, but it is quite another matter if you want to draw a dachshund or a Pekingese. Let's consider the dachshund.

As illustrated above, this small hunting dog has an elongated body and very short legs. Fortunately, because of his slick coat, his structure can be understood easily in direct observation. The all-important position of the elbow is readily apparent. Using the basic forms and a few simple proportional checks, you can quickly establish the identifiable characteristics. Some dachshund proportional checks to look for are: the length of the forelegs from the elbow to the ground is a little less than the depth of the body measured from behind the withers to the underside of the belly. Also, the length of the body, measured from the withers to the tail, is a bit over two times the depth of the body. Such measurements will vary from dog to dog and should be considered only approximate.

Difficulties increase when you are confronted with the task of drawing a small, hairy dog. At first glance some of these little fellows look like nothing so much as an animated dust mop in search of a handle. They are so covered with hair both fore and aft it is difficult to tell if they are coming or going. With a sharp eye you may discover a small dark button at one end of the moving form. This will be the nose. Beneath all the covering you soon discover a fine, friendly pooch with all the structure and character of his bigger brothers.

When drawing such long-haired breeds it may seem futile to worry about their underlying forms. It's not. The best approach is to proceed just as you would for any other animal. Consider a sheep dog: he appears to be nothing but wall-to-wall fuzz. A closer look, however, will show some evidence of the underlying structure. Knowing what that structure must be will help you create a more convincing drawing.

One way to get an understanding of the forms of hairy dogs is to give them a bath. A good soaking will usually mat the fluffy surface of the body, and the real dog is soon apparent.

West Highland White Terrier

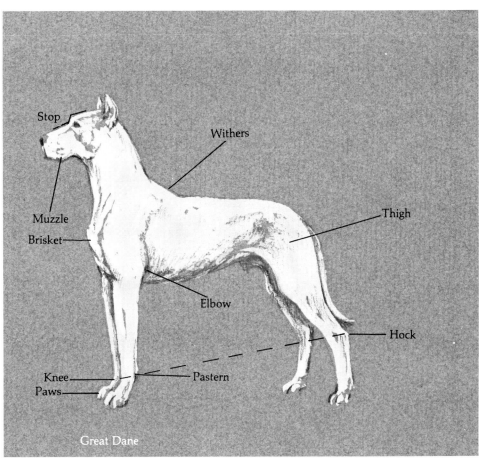

Stop

Withers

Muzzle

Thigh

Brisket

Elbow

Hock

Knee

Pastern

Paws

Great Dane

Names of the parts of the body

From Great Dane to tiny terrier, all dogs are the same in basic structure. No matter what their size or surface covering, they all have similar forms. Also, the names given to the parts of the body are the same.

If you are confused about the location of the elbow and knee, have another look at the skeletons shown on pages 36 and 37. An important point to remember in drawing any dog is that the *knee of the foreleg is always lower than the hock of the hind leg.* (Note broken line on drawing of the Great Dane.) A common mistake many artists make is to suggest the knee and hock are on the same horizontal line. Close observation will show this is not the case in any breed.

Housebook Master (c. 1485) Rijksmuseum, Amsterdam

49

Pointer

Husky

Boxer

Setter

Collie

Shih Tzu

The dog's head

A dog's head is quite as distinctive as his individual proportions or coat. The variety of shapes and sizes is vast, going from the long, pointed nose and narrow head of the whippet or collie to the square, short pug face of a boxer or bulldog. As illustrated here, the length of the nose and the sharpness of the "break" or "stop" is an essential consideration.

Such breeds as setters, pointers, spaniels, huskies, and many hounds have a positive and identifiable stop. Collies, shepherds, many terriers, and a number of the greyhound group have a straighter nose that flows from the forehead with but a minor break; while boxers, English and Boston bulls and the like have short noses and a very abrupt stop. A number of miniature dogs have a sharp break in the nose line although, as with the Shih Tzu, it would take x-ray eyes to see, as the head is almost completely covered with hair.

Close observation and good reference material is necessary to pin down the specific characteristics of a particular breed or type. In general, the nose and head structure of most dogs will be similar to one of the types shown in these sketches.

A

B

C

Details of heads

There is no substitute for observation when you want to make a detailed drawing or painting of a dog's head. As mentioned before, drawing dogs is not easy, because your model has a natural reluctance to hold still. However, even casual observation will tell you the type and relative length of nose, whether the ears stand up or flop, how long they are, etc. With this information and some reference for checks you should be able to get started.

If you are drawing a straight on front view, you'll find it helpful to block in the forms of the head as shown in diagram A. It is wise to establish a center line and a horizontal line to place the eyes. Do this with some deliberation after you have decided on the pose.

Once you have placed the position of the end of the nose on the vertical center line, you can roughly place the eyes on the horizontal line. Diagonal lines drawn from the corners of the nose through the inside corners of the eyes will help in placing the forward base of the ear. This will be the same position whether the ears stand up or hang down.

Blocking-in the head as suggested in diagram B may be helpful when drawing an angled view.

Step C is a sketch of a beagle developed through this blocking-in process. Some photographic reference was also useful. The German shepherd was drawn from life, memory and reference.

A step by step drawing

1   *The initial step is to capture the gesture of the pose—the feeling and rhythm of the action. Keep it free and easy...this pencil drawing is an important step. Try several until you are satisfied. I usually work on visualizing paper.*

2   *I like to work directly over my selected gesture drawing and start to build the form and structure. This is where knowing the basic forms of the animal will help you establish the foreshortening and the feeling of three dimensions.*

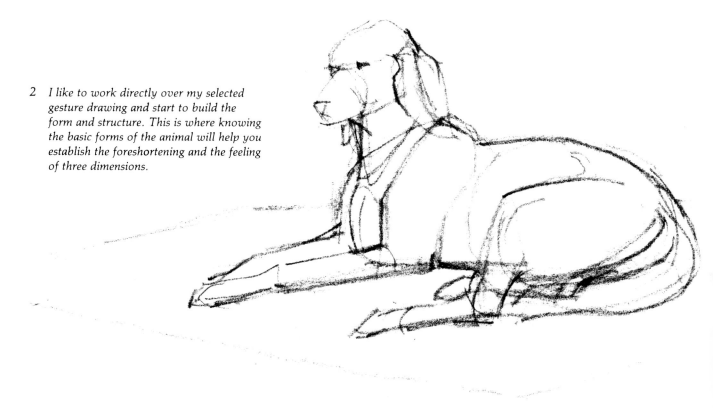

3 Working over the form drawing on another sheet of visualizing paper I begin to think about the surface and the effects of light and shade. In this case the light is planned to come from the upper left.

4 On still another sheet of visualizing paper I begin to refine the light and shadow pattern using a fine felt tip pen. Somewhere along the line I decided the final rendering should be done in scratchboard. Basically, I prefer working from dark to light, particularly when the subject's value is dark. It is also a good medium to use when details of surface texture are important.

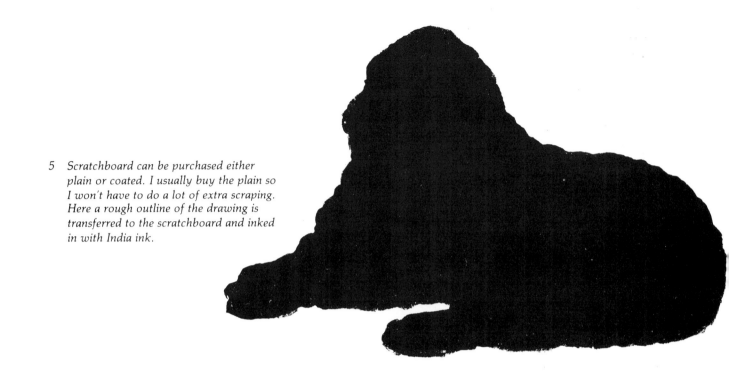

5   Scratchboard can be purchased either
    plain or coated. I usually buy the plain so
    I won't have to do a lot of extra scraping.
    Here a rough outline of the drawing is
    transferred to the scratchboard and inked
    in with India ink.

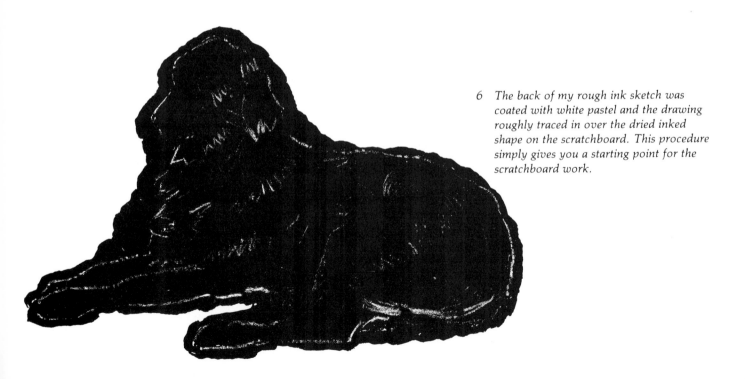

6   The back of my rough ink sketch was
    coated with white pastel and the drawing
    roughly traced in over the dried inked
    shape on the scratchboard. This procedure
    simply gives you a starting point for the
    scratchboard work.

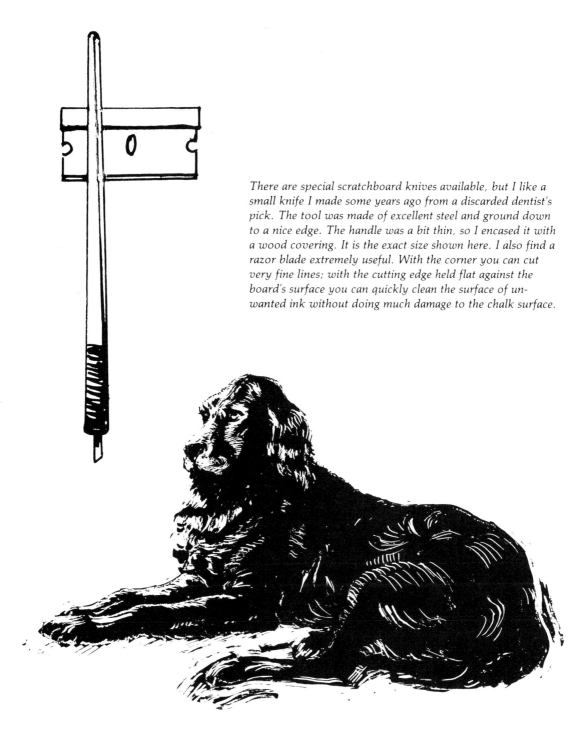

There are special scratchboard knives available, but I like a small knife I made some years ago from a discarded dentist's pick. The tool was made of excellent steel and ground down to a nice edge. The handle was a bit thin, so I encased it with a wood covering. It is the exact size shown here. I also find a razor blade extremely useful. With the corner you can cut very fine lines; with the cutting edge held flat against the board's surface you can quickly clean the surface of unwanted ink without doing much damage to the chalk surface.

7　This step shows the process of starting to draw with the knife. Try to keep in mind the direction of the forms and the flow of the surface texture. At this stage the pen drawing serves as the best guide.

8 *Many people think a scratchboard rendering must be done in a mechanical manner. I believe it can be more loosely handled and still be effective. You can work back into the drawing to correct areas by carefully re-inking areas with a small brush. Wait until it dries, then scratch again. Don't count on being able to do this too often in one spot. In this drawing I reworked parts of the dog's head three times. You can also cover scratched lines or reduce their intensity by crosshatching with a pen or small, pointed brush and ink. You can see where this was done on the rear legs and tail.*

Every artist approaches the subject in his own way.

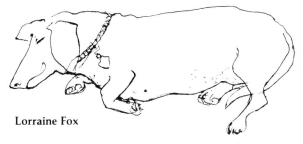

Lorraine Fox

The artist's accurate eye and sensitive line allow the form and character of this sleeping dog to show with a simple outline approach.

Harold Von Schmidt

Von Schmidt has a wonderful sense and knowledge of animal forms. This pointer is simply and accurately stated. Notice the way the hind legs are turned and the foreshortening suggested.

J. C. Leyendecker
This fine draughtsman painted animals as he did everything else — with style, sureness and verve.

57

Gustave Courbet

St. Louis City Art Museum

*This 19th century French artist's Greyhounds are
rather different than the Dürer drawing on page 39.
Yet, in both cases, notice how the form and structure
are amply apparent.*

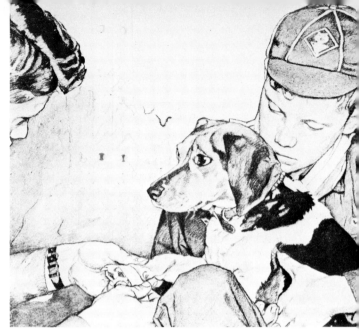

Norman Rockwell

*Few artists understood the importance of dogs to the
human condition better than Rockwell. Usually dogs
played a supporting role in the scene, but they contrib-
uted greatly to the final effect.*

George F. Goodyear and the Buffalo Fine Arts Academy

Giacomo Balla

*This Futurist painting does a fine job of
capturing the feeling of a small dog in motion.*

Paul Bransom

*This noted draughtsman had a fine career as a wild
illustrator. Most of his works were black and white
tonal drawings in pencil or charcoal.*

Cats 4

"The artist does not draw what he sees,
but what he must make others see."

Edgar Degas (1834-1917)

Have you ever noticed how often you see pictures of a cat or kittens on magazine covers? A cursory survey will reveal cats hold the showplace of honor almost as frequently as pretty girls. And for good reason. An editor of a popular publication told me having a cat illustration on the cover is a sure way to increase newsstand sales.

There is little doubt cats have wide appeal, but, in fact, their veneration is something less than universal. There is no middle ground with cats. Most people think they are great and the epitome of animal life. Others, however, feel quite the other way and are not comfortable around any aloof and arrogant feline. Cats, the smartest of all domesticated animals, probably sense a negative attitude and respond in kind. Whether you like cats or can do without them, their form and grace make them a pleasure and challenge to draw or paint.

Chronologically, members of the cat family have been around a long time. While the dog as a recognized species goes back a mere 15 million years, the cat's ancestor, the weasel-like Miacis, is said to have prowled the earth 50 million years ago; and cats as we know them today have been going their own way for some 40 million years.

The ancient Egyptians are given the credit for first domesticating the household cat. They successfully tamed the small wild felines and used them to guard their granaries from the infestation of mice and rats. The cats did such a good job they became a part of Egyptian lore and were even worshipped as gods. (The goddess Bebastis who represented the sun had the head of a cat.) Some beautiful Egyptian sculptures of cats and jewelry with cat motifs have survived over 4000 years.

From Egypt domesticated cats spread throughout the world and have been closely associated with man in every land and every climate. Along the way cats have become omens of fortune, both for good or ill, and part of the folklore of most cultures.

A cat was the symbol of liberty in ancient Rome. Sailors once believed a cat aboard their ship would bring good luck to a voyage. Yet, many know black cats are unlucky, and beware if one crosses in front of you! *Cats* are said to possess nine lives. Also, we're sure you can be someone's *cat's* paw; you can let the *cat* out of the bag, and certainly curiosity killed a *cat*...As with dogs, cats are an integral part of our lives and heritage. Like them or not, it would be a poorer world without them.

The cat family embraces a great variety of re-

markable animals. Besides the ubiquitous house pet, there are lions, panthers, leopards, tigers, jaguars, cheetahs, lynx, wildcats, ocelots, cougars and more. They are all smart, clever, patient, powerful and quick. Some, such as the cheetah, are, for short distances, among the fastest animals in the world.

Domestic cats are classified into a number of breeds, each having characteristic features. They are also grouped according to color and markings. The short-haired cats include: Siamese, Burmese, Russian Blue, Havana Brown, Manx (no tail), Rex, and Domestic Shorthair. Long-haired breeds are Persian, Angora, Himalayan, and other rare types.

Although the range in size from a small alley cat to a lion is substantial, all have the same type skeletal formation, with the same kind of suppleness and pattern of movement. In short, whether you are drawing a domestic short-haired cat or a cougar, the structure will be the same. Differences exist in characteristics of the head, tail, surface covering and proportions. The important thing is to try to capture the spirit and grace of movement so apparent in all cats. If you wish to draw a specific type, be sure to do some research to acquaint yourself with their special characteristics.

In general, cats make better models than dogs, but even under the best of circumstances they will move more than you would like. Draw as much as you can from direct observation. *Look* as you draw so your eyes and mind come to sense the forms and characteristics. Drawing short-haired cats will make it easier to understand the construction and proportions. When you are drawing cats with long hair, keep in mind the underlying structure. It is hard to see, but it is there. Knowing what is underneath will help you better interpret the surface.

A 15-inch high Egyptian bronze statuette of a cat said to date circa 330 B.C.

Alfred Chadbourn

The flexible cat

Cats are the most flexible of four-legged animals and they can, and do, assume some wierd and wonderful poses. The reason for this is their bone structure. It is quite unique. Compared to the dog, horse, cow and nearly all other four-legged animals, members of the cat family can move, twist, and bend with amazing agility. Their secret is simple. They have a short, tapered rib cage with a relatively longer, more flexible spine. Because of the size and shape of the rib basket their shoulders are less restricted in lateral movement.

Compare the two diagrams at the right. The cat and dog are drawn at about the same size for the sake of comparison. The shape of the rib basket is blacked-in for visual clarity.

The cat and dog have the same number of ribs, but the basket formation of the cat is relatively smaller, both in length and in depth, than that of the dog or other animals. Notice in the diagram how the rib cage of the dog obstructs the legs' sideways movement (point A), while the shape of the cat's offers no such obstruction. For this reason the cat is able to move his forelegs from side to side in a crossing action which a dog and the others cannot achieve. This is one of the reasons a cat can climb so well. With sharp claws, the ability to wrap his front legs around the trunk, and powerful hind legs, cats have little trouble scaling almost any tree.

If you have ever seen a bucking bronco or a rodeo bull in action you know these animals have a mighty range of movement with their hind legs. So do the dog and other animals, but the cat, because of his greater relative length of spine, has even greater versatility of movement in the hind quarters.

The old cliche', "as agile as a cat," succinctly says it all.

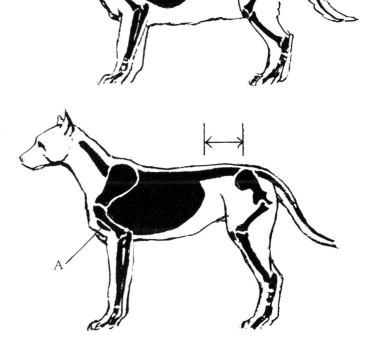

Simplified forms of a cat

The proportional differences between the cat and the dog are considerable. Their basic forms, however, are similar. Most of the cat's structure can be simplified with modified cylinders, as illustrated.

The smaller members of the cat family have a rather round head with but a small break at the brow, making the profile slightly convex. When drawing the head of a house cat, you can begin with a sphere and fasten a conical shape to it for the nose and muzzle structure. This should occupy the lower third of the head form. In larger cats such as lions or tigers, the nose is proportionally bigger and the forehead is less arched.

The cat's body, from house pet to panther, is a long modified cylinder over which the wedge forms of the shoulders and the hind quarters overlap. The legs, neck and even the tail are all cylindrical.

Knowing these forms and the simplified skeleton (see page 63) will help when you are lost in the wilderness of a fuzzy, long-haired cat, or when faced with a difficult foreshortening problem.

1

2

3

4

5

6

Walk

All members of the cat family walk in a sequence similar to dogs and most other four-legged animals. From direct observation it is difficult to discern a time when three legs do not appear to be on the ground at once. However, with high speed photographs or slow motion movies, positions such as 2 and 5 are evident where but two legs support the weight at a given moment.

Close observation shows the front leg moves forward and touches the ground just after the back leg on the same side. As pointed out earlier, the back paw often lands exactly on the spot the front paw, on the same side, has just occupied. Thus, if you were able to track a cat (or many other animals) on wet ground, you are likely to see but two footprints in a stride sequence. In faster gaits there may be some foot slippage, but the same overlapping pattern usually occurs.

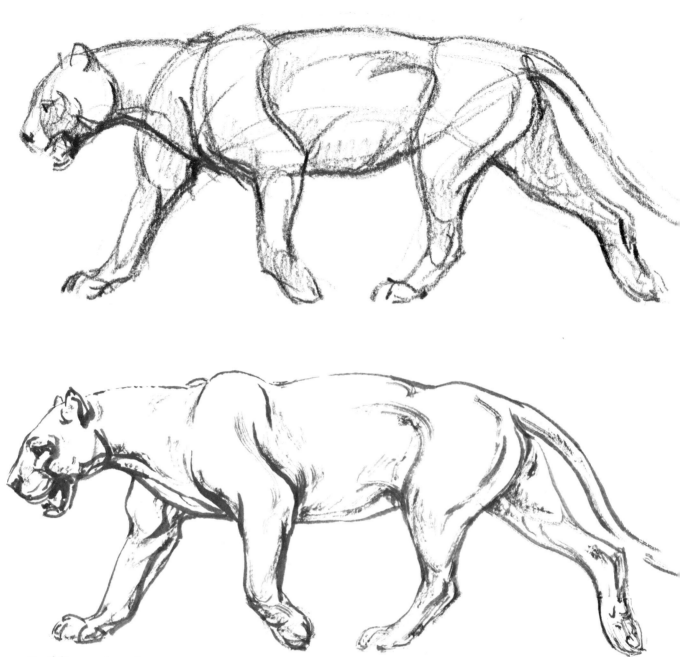

Building a drawing

The top sketch, done in grease pencil, shows the development of the modified animal forms directly over a gesture drawing. Note the flow of line from the head to the tail, and from the legs through the body.

In the brush and ink drawing below, the lines were simplified without losing the rhythm of the action or the feeling of the bulk and form.

No matter whether the cat is large or small, the fluidity of line and pattern of movement remains the same.

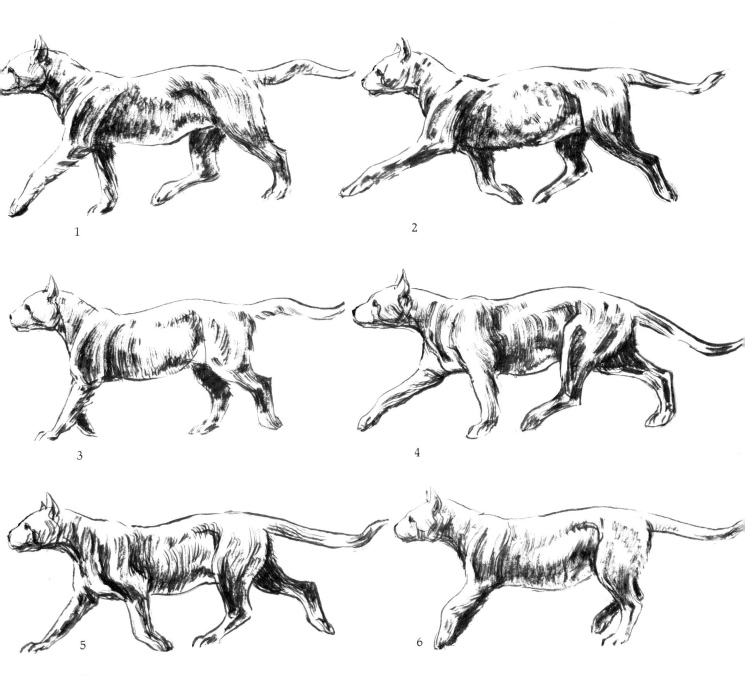

1

2

3

4

5

6

Trot

Cats trot in the same manner as most other four-footed animals. It is a diagonal movement. The front and rear legs on opposite sides move together, i.e., the right front leg moves forward at the same time as the left rear, and the left front and right rear legs move forward together. By observation it appears two legs are always on the ground. However, the camera will show what our eyes cannot perceive: at the instant of maximum extension all four paws are briefly off the ground at once. These positions are illustrated in positions 2 and 5.

Harold Von Schmidt

In this detail of a brush and ink illustration Von again demonstrates his fund of animal knowledge. The poised, mid-air position of the mountain lion's legs, extended claws, head down and ears back, leave the viewer in no doubt what is about to happen to the cat's unlucky victim. Here it is all accurately stated with a minimum of means.

Gallop

All animals do not gallop in the same way. Cats gallop quite differently than dogs. As already noted the dog, deer, antelope, elk and a few others, gallop with a rotary leg sequence. Most other animals, including the cat family, employ a transverse or diagonal gallop.

In any galloping action the animal's legs are alternately stretched out and brought under the body, creating a fore and aft, up and down rocking motion. By observation it often seems at least two feet are on the ground at a time, but actually, most of the time the weight is carried by only one leg. At intervals in this gait all four legs are off the ground at once.

The diagrams 1 through 4 at the right show the cat's foot sequence as the weight is shifted from leg to leg. First the right front leg is down, next the left rear, then the right rear and finally the left front. The sequence is then repeated.

Cats, for maximum speed, often incorporate in their orthodox gallop a spring or leaping motion. This is seldom a continuous leaping action such as deer or sheep might employ, but rather it is a combination of a leap and a gallop. This is how it works: there is a slight hesitation as the cat comes to position 2 and both hind feet land and assume a springing position. This is illustrated in 2A. 3A shows the mid-air leap and the landing follows as shown in position 4. In this stance the cat can continue with the normal gallop or repeat the leaping action.

In all these sketches note that the cat's ears are drawn in a back position. Cats often gallop or leap with their ears erect, but a frightened cat or one about to enter a fight will put its ears back. Small details such as this sometimes add flavor and believability to a drawing.

1

2

2a

3

3a

4

1 3
4 2

69

Hints on drawing the head

From a straight on front view a cat's head appears like a slightly flattened sphere on which a small, tapered cylinder is attached to form the nose and muzzle. It helps to establish vertical and horizontal center lines for the placement of the eyes and nose. The horizontal line must be raised or lowered, depending on your eye level. The more you are above the cat the lower the eye line will appear; the lower your vantage point the higher the line. This is assuming, of course, the cat is holding his head in a stationary position—an unlikely assumption.

Once you have determined the position of the nose and the eyes, the ears can be placed by drawing slightly curved lines from the corners of the nose through the corners of the eyes and extending the lines about three quarters up the head. This is the approximate position for the base of the ears.

The ears are set on the head at an angle and should be about the width of the base of the ear apart.

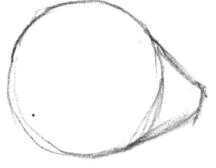

In a profile view you can again start with the slightly flattened sphere, with the small cylinder form for the nose and muzzle. The eyes should be located about one-third the length of the head up from the nose. Remember the eyes are recessed in a protective socket and are quite large in relation to the size of the head. The base of the ear is curved and starts about three quarters the length of the head back from the nose. Indications of fur and details should be added only after you understand the underlying structure.

Cats have large eyes, and in strong light the iris contracts to a small sliver as shown. As the light decreases the iris opens up greatly and becomes large and round.

Rosa Bonheur
Lion's Head (detail)

This French artist was extremely popular during her lifetime, but her star faded soon after her death in '99. Despite the fickleness of fame, some of her animal drawings are outstanding.

Charles Livingston Bull
Leopard (detail)

Eugene Delacroix
Head of a Lion, Profile

Step by step rendering in wash

I've often thought Murphy must have been engaged in doing a wet-in-wet wash when he propounded his famous law: *If anything can go wrong, it will.* The soft edges and delightful accidents that occur with this tricky technique can be a joy when all goes well. Unfortunately, the chance of immediate success is remote, particularly if you are dealing with a subject requiring some control, such as rendering an animal. This demonstration is a case in point. The final painting, as shown in Step 5, represents the fourth try at achieving something close to the version I had in mind. After my third failure I

was convinced wet-in-wet should remain the exclusive possession of the landscape painter, where the capricious flow of water and pigment can have its own way in creating sky, clouds, water, and foliage effects. Here is the blow by blow account of fighting this reluctant feline into existence.

No definite model was used. The drawing evolved out of a number of direct observation sketches I made of cats in a variety of poses several years ago. I had in mind a big, blue-gray, battle-scarred tomcat who has that disdainful, no illusions, I've-seen-it-all look.

1   Since the pose was not a duplication of any of my sketches, I started as usual with a simple gesture sketch. It took several attempts to arrive at a satisfactory pose.

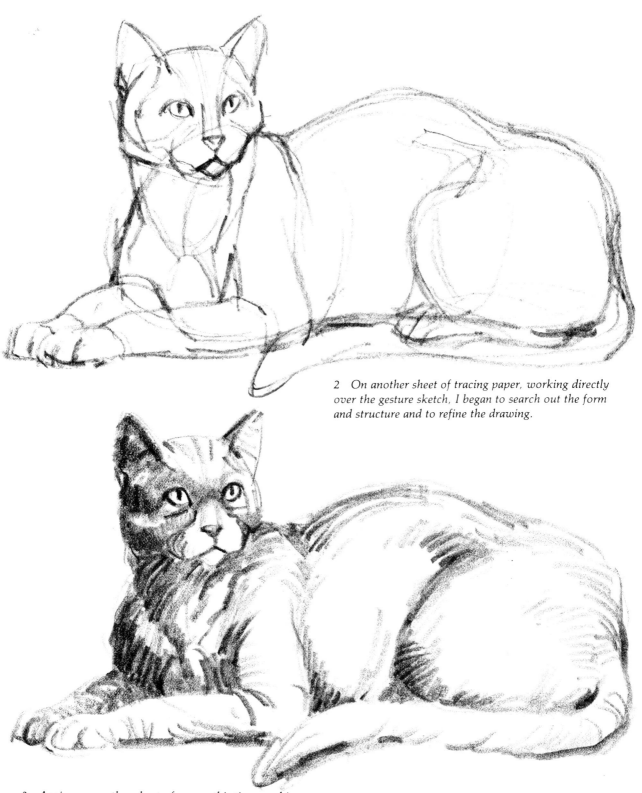

2   On another sheet of tracing paper, working directly over the gesture sketch, I began to search out the form and structure and to refine the drawing.

3   Again, on another sheet of paper, this time working over the form drawing, I began to develop a broad light and dark pattern. Since I had a loose wash inter-pretation in mind for the final rendering, I tried to keep the values simple and uncomplicated.

4   The sketch made in step 2 was roughly traced onto a sheet of Arches mounted cold pressed watercolor paper. Up to now everything was progressing nicely.

Since my goal was a blue-gray cat, my palette was limited to Payne's gray and ivory black. Next, the paper was thoroughly wet with a #26 watercolor brush, and it was allowed to dry for several minutes. Exactly how long you should let paper dry is difficult to tell. In this case I tested a touch of color on the edge of the paper with a brush loaded with Payne's gray wash. The test bled considerably, but not too much to control, and I judged the right degree of dampness had arrived.

With a #8 sable brush I quickly established the dark areas of the cat with a middle value of Payne's gray. The purpose was to create a soft, fuzzy edge. My pencil value sketch (step 3) was used as reference.

At this point in the final rendering (three earlier attempts had already gone sour) I discovered my paper had several razor cuts in the surface which I had not noticed until the wash found its way into the incisions, creating some unwanted dark vertical lines. I hoped the addition of darker values might cover them, so I proceeded.

5 I continued to build up the values, working as much as possible on damp surfaces. As the paper became too dry I rewet the area carefully with clear water and a clean brush. Occasionally it was necessary to blot too damp an area with a soft rag or tissue.

A mixture of black and Payne's gray was used for the eyes and a few accents on the face, chest, elbow, shoulder, hip and tail. The work on the face was done with glazes of value, working mainly on a dry surface.

When dry the fuzzy wet-in-wet areas around the head and back seemed too pronounced. To overcome this I wet the background with clean water, and when I gauged the degree of dampness was right I stabbed in a swatch of Payne's gray above the cat's back. The color quickly fanned out into the shape you see. Small touches of gray were added to the wet area in front of the cat as well as at the rear. The addition of the wash background also suggests an environment for the cat which seems helpful.

After the entire surface was completely dry a few highlights in the muzzle, eyes, and shoulder area were scratched out with a razor blade. In a few places an ink eraser was lightly used for minor value adjustments. The whiskers were scratched in with the tip of a razor. Finally, a few touches of opaque were used to match the wash values and eliminate the last vestiges of the unwanted vertical cut lines.

The reproduction is about 25% smaller than the original.

Cats interpreted by a variety of artists

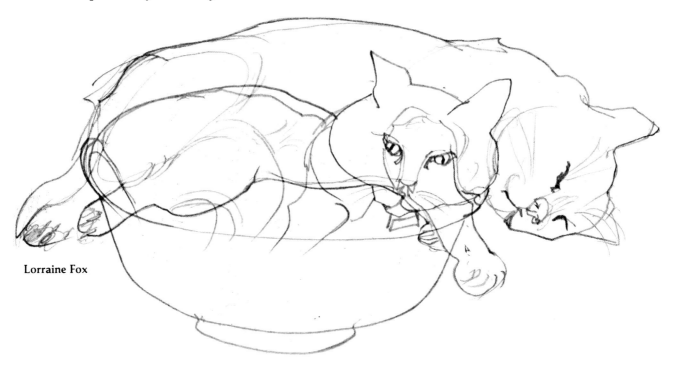

Lorraine Fox

Unknown artist
Japanese print, date unknown

Eugene Delacroix
Tiger (detail)

Louvre Museum, Paris

Austin Briggs

Robert Fawcett

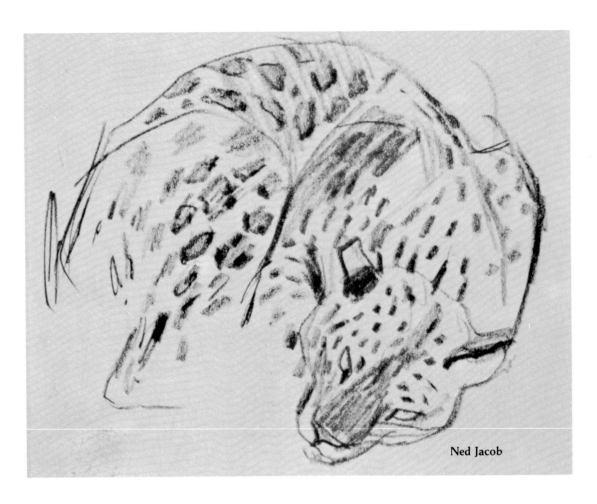

Ned Jacob

The contrast of approaches between the formally designed, accurately delineated tiger by the American wildlife illustrator shown at the right, and the interpretation by the noted Austrian Expressionist (far right), is dramatic. Most observers will find Bull's picture more understandable as it is based on tradition and what is generally considered real. Kokoschka's painting, however, deserves thoughtful consideration. Instead of reality, the artist was trying to project a feeling—the growl and fearsomeness, if you will, of a savage beast, rather than his physical likeness. There is validity in both approaches.

Charles Livingston Bull

Ben Stahl

Oskar Kokoschka

Benjamin Scharps and David Scharps Fund
Museum of Modern Art, New York

Rembrandt
Lion resting, Pen and brush with brown ink

Horses **5**

"I guess I broke more horses' legs in my
drawings than all the gopher holes in the state
of Montana, but, by golly, my hoss would move."

Charles M. Russell (1864-1926)
as quoted by Harold Von Schmidt

In the 1920's the famed cowboy artist Charlie Russell wrote: "A few years ago a hoss was considered kind of handy to have around. He was needed everywhere and used all ways. Up hill or down, mud or dust, he worked. They made no good roads for him. There's not a city in mighty near the whole world he didn't help build. There's a few ice-bound countries where the hoss don't live, and in these same lands it ain't easy for humans to live."*

It is sobering to consider what a short time ago it was when society was deeply dependent on the sound wind and stout limbs and faithful service of the horse to make the wheels of civilization go around. The ascendancy of the automobile and other appurtenances of industrial technology make our way of life much different than that of our ancestors. If we live in the Age of the Car, truly, our forbears lived in the Age of the Horse.

For thousands of years horses served as the major means of land transportation, communication, and the performers of heavy labor. They plowed the fields, hauled the produce, pulled the carriages, brought the firewagons, herded the cattle, carried the mail, went to war and, on holidays, ran races. Not many of us would want to forego the "necessities" and comforts technology offers, but most of us recognize our machine-borne benefits do not totally compensate for some of our losses. Not the least of our forfeited inheritance has to do with the diminished status of the horse. Consider these parallels and decide which is more appealing: a cattleman in a pick-up truck versus a cowboy on his pony; a diesel tractor plowing a field or team of horses doing the job; a fume-spewing taxi or a horse-drawn hansom cab; a column of clanking armored vehicles or a troop of cavalry on parade.

The utility, stamina, heroics, and beauty of the horse are legend. Even in his present status limited largely to play and luxury, the noble steed's position in our culture is secure. The names: Black Beauty, Smokey, Silver, Tony, Trigger, Twenty Grand, Man o' War, Citation, Secretariat—to cite but a few—are as much a part of American folklore as Davy Crockett or Babe Ruth.

A hundred years ago the common saying, "A man on foot is no man at all," was not a frivolous reference to a hitchhiker. In many parts of the country it was a truthful condition relating to a per-

son unfortunate enough to be without a horse. At the time it was also understood and plausible to suggest, "A man is no better than his horse." Even today we are dependent on "horsepower," but what we mean is a machine calibrated to lift a specified number of 550 foot-pounds per second. Other phrases remain in our vocabulary such as: *working like a horse, horse sense, horse opera, iron horse, frisky as a colt*...The horse is still with us in sport and spirit, although his numbers are decreasing rapidly. At the turn of the century there were about 20 million horses in America; now there are less than 4 million.

Scientists tell us the ancestors of the horse can be traced back about 60 million years. During his development astounding physical changes took place. The most notable alterations were in size, tooth structure, and foot formation. Apparently the founder of the line was a little rabbit-like creature called Hyracotherium. Succeeding millennia produced an animal about the size of a small dog with laterally directed eyes and padded feet having four toes on each front foot and three on each hind foot. The tips of the toes were tiny hoofs. This fellow is called Eohippus. He was followed by Miohippus who was about as big as a good-sized dog, having long slender legs, and each foot had three toes. The next stage is known as Parahippus whose skull closely resembled the modern horse. He still had lateral vision, but the position of his eyes allowed for more forward vision. Mesohippus, or middle horse, came next and he lived 30 million years ago.

The modern horse as we know him came on the scene about a million years ago. In the evolution his side toes became bones along the legs, leaving a single strong center hoof. Also, the teeth were better formed for eating grass.

It is interesting to note fossil remains of early stages of the horse have been found in every continent except Australia. Scientists speculate the Western Hemisphere was probably the birthplace of equine existence. Yet, by the time of the discovery of the New World there were no horses here. In fact, one of the reasons small forces of conquistadores were able to conquer great Indian civilizations was because the Spanish had a few horses. The Indians, never having seen a horse, thought horse and rider to be one unified, terrifying beast. In time they learned the difference and discovered a stolen horse would carry an Indian as effectively as a Spaniard.

*From "Trails Plowed Under" by Charles M. Russell ©1927. Printed with permission of the Estate of Nancy C. Russell.

Why the horse did not remain or survive in its place of origin is not known. Equus prospered and multiplied in many other parts of the world and is first thought to have been tamed by prehistoric Indo-Europeans. (Drawings from that area over 5000 years old show men mounted on horses.) The fact remains the horse was re-introduced to the Americas by way of the Spanish and other Europeans.

Through escape and abandonment the big European horses, bred to carry the heavy load of a soldier in armor, grew into the herds of small, hardy mustangs that roamed the plains, with the result the life of the Western Indian was inexorably changed. Within a few generations the pedestrian tribes of the plains became some of the best horsemen in the world.

Although all modern horses are of the family Equus, there exist vast differences in their sizes and characteristics. The range from a Shetland pony to a Clydesdale is roughly equivalent as that of a Pomeranian to a Great Dane. The problem of drawing the horse, however, is simpler than with the many-faceted canine; but for the artist the distinctive features of the horse may cause more trouble. Here is why: horses are so large they often occupy major portions of the picture area. Their size makes them difficult to hide or disguise. Facts, details, and subtle variations cannot be obscured or ignored. Another consideration, this one having mixed blessings, is that people love horses and almost everyone loves pictures of them. Because of this interest and high esteem many individuals know a great deal about horses. Any artist who wants to draw and paint them successfully had better know what he is doing. A mistake in the rendering of a horse galls a knowledgeable person the way a misspelled word on a billboard horrifies an orthographer. For all of these reasons we will discuss and examine the special characteristics and nuances of horses in greater detail than other animals.

Shoulder structure

The diagrams at the right show front view sections of the shoulder formations as they exist in man and the horse.

The human shoulder blades run across the back and are held in position by the clavicles. Without clavicles the shoulders of animals slide downward alongside the rib cage. Note that the rib structure of man is relatively wide from side to side in relation to his size.

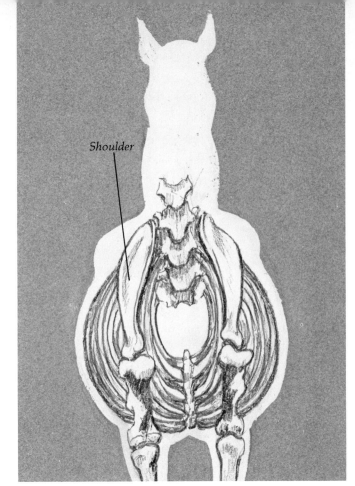

Horse

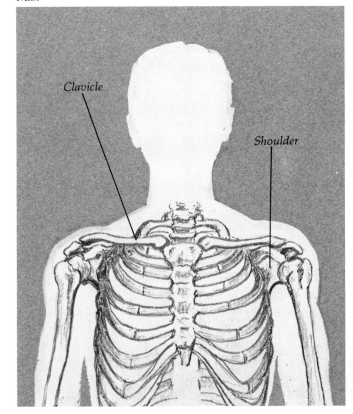

Man

These drawings are not in size relationship.

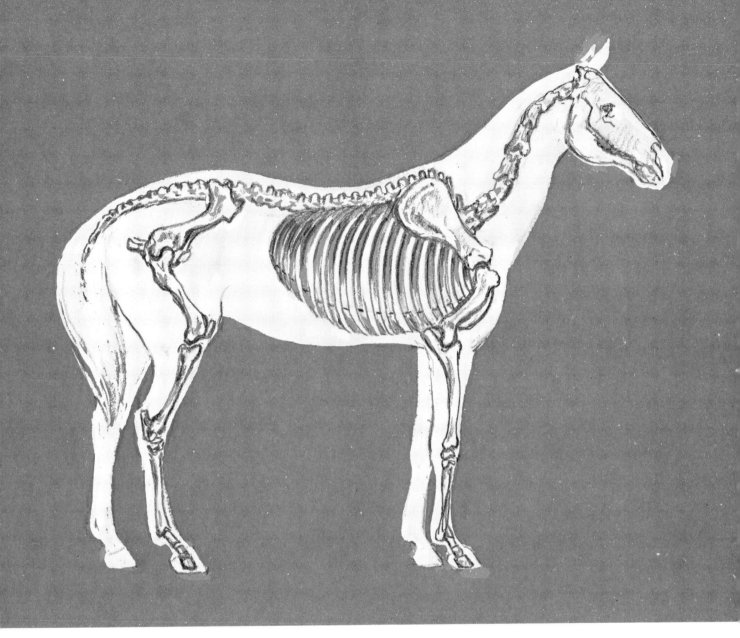

Basic structure

A glance back at page 36 will show the skeleton of the horse to be remarkably like that of the dog except for the differences in the feet, position of the neck, and the formation of the mouth and jaw. Because of their structural similarity, the range of movement of the horse and dog is also about the same. Notice how the positions of the rib cage and the breastbone restrict the lateral movement of the front legs of the horse, just as the bones in the same area limit the action of the dog (See page 63). The hind legs of both animals have a much greater range of movement, allowing them to twist and kick sideways most effectively.

The lower position of the neck bones makes it possible for the horse to keep his head down for grazing over long periods without the discomfort of having to bend or splay his front legs.

Since the horse is a vegetarian, his teeth are different than carnivorous animals. The horse's front teeth are the choppers that cut off the grass while the back teeth are effective grinders. Unlike the bovine family, the horse has both upper and lower front teeth, and is capable of inflicting a powerful bite. Horses seldom hold their mouths open as dogs do when hot because horses sweat through the pores of their skins just as we do. Dogs perspire through their mouths.

Another important characteristic of a horse is his eyes. Compared to most other animals, they are large and are placed so he can see a large semicircle on each side of his head. This is the reason horses are often fitted with blinders in races. Restricting their vision so they can see only the area in front of them sometimes helps to keep them from becoming skittish or distracted.

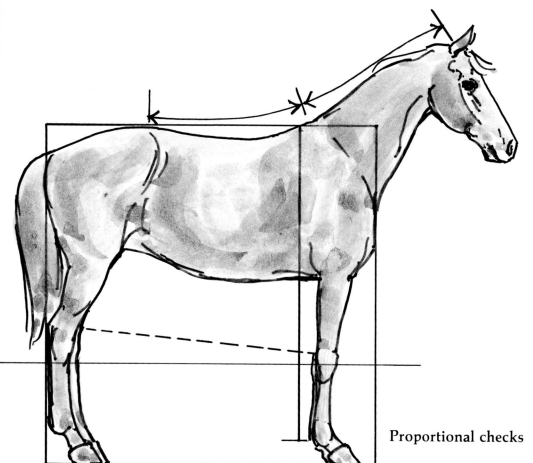

The point of studying and comparing skeletons is not to emphasize the technical or clinical aspects of animal drawing. The purpose is to show the similarities in animals and humans so you can apply knowledge you already know to drawing problems you will encounter. For instance: Suppose you are in doubt as to what direction the pastern of a horse's front foot would be able to move. You might find the answer if you could observe a horse first hand, or maybe you would be lucky and find some evidence in your reference file. Both solutions are not always possible, and both can consume much time.

The other approach is to apply information you already have about human forms and relate that knowledge to the equivalent area of the animal you are drawing. By knowing the pastern of the horse's front leg corresponds to the four fingers of the hand, and the fetlock is the knuckle joint, you will be able to determine the kind of movement the animal could achieve. If you hold your fingers rigidly together, and press down on a table top so that the weight is on your fingernails, you will have a situation similar to a horse's foot. It should then be apparent how the hinge action of the fetlock (knuckles) allows an up and down movement, but little or no sideways action.

Proportional checks

Here are some basic measurements for an "average" horse. After you learn them we'll take up a few exceptions for special types of horses. You will be surprised, however, how often these checks hold true. It is important to keep in mind these measurements only work when the horse is seen at a straight on side view. As soon as any foreshortening is involved the measurements become a matter of estimate. However, knowing the side view measurements will give you a better basis on which to base your judgement of the foreshortening.

• The body and legs fit into a square. Pay particular attention to how the square is formed, where and what parts of the body touch the sides.
• The length of the foreleg from the fetlock to the underside of the belly measures about the same length as the depth of the body taken from the high point of the withers directly down to the lower part of the barrel of the body.
• The distance from the top of the skull to the high point of the withers is about the same as the distance from the same point on the withers to the high point of the hip.
• The length of the head is just about the same as the depth of the body.
• As already mentioned concerning the dog, the knee of the foreleg is definitely lower than the hock of the hind leg.

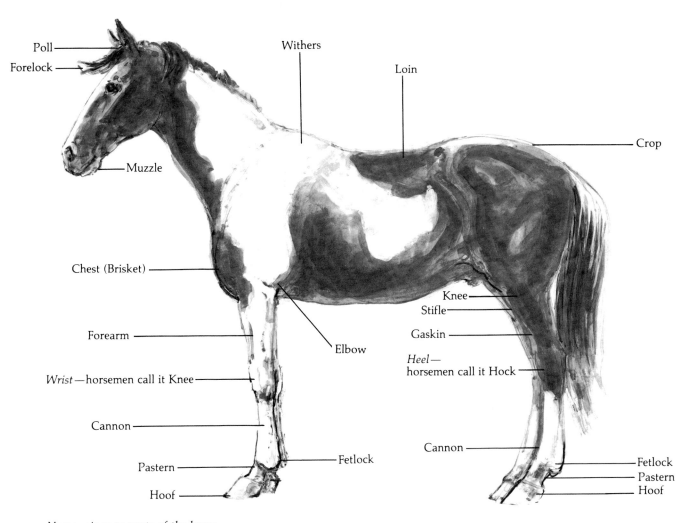

Names given to parts of the horse

Many of the names horsemen apply to a horse are logical and consistent with names given similar parts of other species. Some are confusing, particularly if you want to compare true bone relationships. For instance, it is called the knee of the foreleg of a horse, but if we relate that section to our own skeleton it is obvious the accurate title would be wrist. *Also, the hock of the hind leg would be more properly called the* ankle. *Such refinements are necessary to understand skeletal relationships, but don't use these terms around horse people. They would think you were crazy.*

Personal reflection

The model for this drawing was our family's horse. His name was Flash; he stood 14.2 hands and weighed about 900 pounds. His name would suggest speed, but that was wishful thinking when he was named. As far as is known he never ran in any kind of a race; if he had surely he would have lost. His heart wasn't in such nonsense. His conformation was something short of regal, and his training left gaps big enough for him to walk through. Once he competed in a horse show; a 4-H jamboree in which he, and my son (his rider), won a large green rib-bon in one event. It was for 6th place. There were six horses entered. But, to our family Flash was the smartest, most remarkable horse in the world. There is no doubt about that.

He would have been better named Houdini as he was a true escape artist. There wasn't a fence made that could hold him unless he decided he wanted to stay. Fortunately, such was usually the case. A roaming horse can be a nuisance anywhere, in a suburban community the effect can be devastating. Flash was a dedicated explorer, and his expeditions usually took place in the middle of the night. He had a passion for looking in neighbors' windows. You can imagine the reaction when his presence became known about 2 A.M.

By most standards Flash's accomplishments were small. He caused a fair amount of mischief and went his own way. He was stubborn—he was also patient. He never hurt anyone, and though frequently surrounded by youngsters he never stepped on a child. To avoid doing so at times required standing with a foot poised in mid-air like a trained Lipizzan. He seemed to like us. We certainly liked him. When he died at 32 he was sorely missed. He still is.

Pieter Bruegel the Elder
Rider and Two Horses

This beautiful drawing done nearly 500 years ago is a fine example of accurate observation and sensitive treatment. Isn't it interesting that this Flemish Master's rendering of what must have been a common type horse of the day conforms almost exactly to the proportional guidelines just covered? Yet, these same precepts will work when drawing horses of perhaps less character, but more regal conformations.

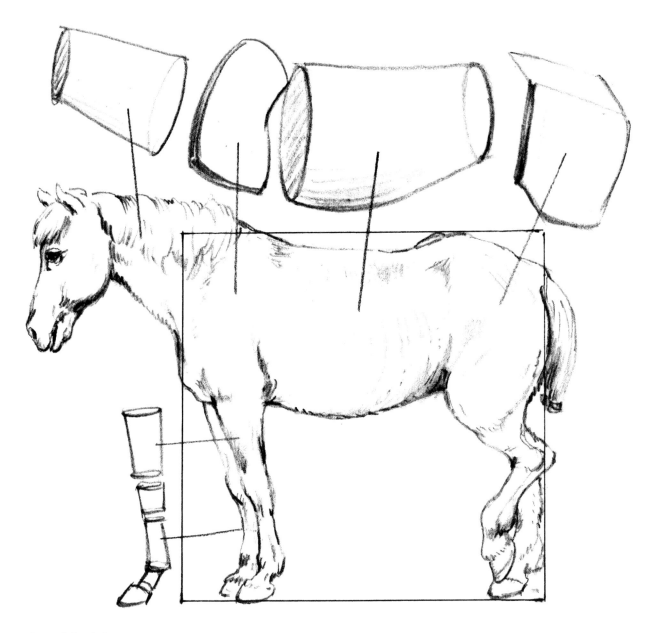

Simplified forms

With apologies to Bruegel, here is a tracing of his horse sans rider and harness. Notice how the body and legs conform to the square and the other proportional measurements discussed on the previous pages. The distance from the back of the head to the high point of the withers equals the measure from the withers to the hip. The head is about the same length as the depth of the body; and the length of the foreleg from the fetlock to the belly is nearly equal to the body depth measured from the withers.

With little excess line, this drawing also clearly shows the basic forms of the horse. The pull-outs indicate how the simplified cylinders of the neck, body, and legs are much the same as those of the cat and dog. In a similar way, the wedge forms of the shoulders and hips fit over the barrel of the body. The head is a modified cylindrical form, but we will go into that in more detail later when we'll also consider the special character of the pastern, fetlock and hoof.

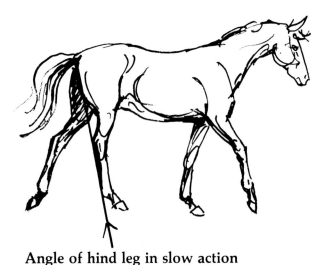

Angle of hind leg in slow action

Careful observation of the horse walking or in many other non-extreme actions will show that a line drawn along the back of the weight-bearing hind leg will, when

extended, lead to the base of the tail. This is demonstrated in the two drawings above. Utilizing such information will help you avoid positioning the weight-bearing leg at a false angle.

Gaits of a horse

The multiplicity of names ascribed to the various speeds of a horse's locomotion can be confusing. Like most animals, horses have three basic gaits: walk, trot, and gallop. Frequently, however, horses are trained to do additional gaits such as the pace. Also, the five-gaited show horse will perform the three natural gaits plus a rack and a slow gait. The definition of these two additional gaits varies somewhat from one locality to another. The special qualities involved in the pace, rack, and slow gait are covered on page 94.

Some other terms you hear relating to a horse's action are:

Amble—a slow pace in which the legs move forward in lateral pairs but not simultaneously. When properly performed a four-beat rhythm is created as each foot hits the ground separately. The same gait is also referred to as *singlefoot* or *slowgait*.

Tennessee Walking Horse is a specially trained saddle horse with a very comfortable fast walk.

Canter—a slow, easy gallop where the legs are not extended for full speed.

Lope—a leisurely gallop with long strides.

Walk

Most four-legged animals walk in a similar manner. Basically the horse walks exactly as the dog or cat, as examined earlier. Often in a stride sequence three feet are on the ground at once. At times, as shown in positions 2, 3, and 6, but two legs are touching the ground. As you can see, however, one leg in each case is just about to land.

When any animal moves in any gait there is always more than a direct forward motion. Slight side to side and up and down movement always occurs as the animal shifts weight from leg to leg. Such movement is necessary to maintain balance. The head and tail are a part of this regular motion pattern. As any rider knows, a horse's head, particularly in a walk, moves up and down and from side to side slightly with each step. Suggesting this kind of minor movement will make your drawing more convincing. In the sketches on the opposite page, note the tail positions and the head movement shown in positions 3 and 6.

1

2

3

4

5

6

Trot

Just as with the dog and cat, the horse trots by moving the legs on the opposite sides of his body in reciprocal action with each other. As you can see in the drawings, the right front leg moves forward at the same time as the left rear; and the left front moves forward with the right rear. There are times during a fast trot when all four legs will be off the ground at once. This is shown in position 3.

The distance the horse's feet are lifted off the ground will vary. Often the feet seem to barely clear the ground. Show horses, however, are often trained to move with a more exaggerated leg action.

The diagonal motion of this gait is not a comfortable ride, but a well-conditioned horse can cover long distances in a trot at a fast, even clip. Trotters trained for harness racing make impressive speeds. This is rather remarkable when you consider the trot is not the animal's natural gait for full speed.

In photographs that freeze an action it is sometimes difficult to identify the difference between a walk and a trot. For this reason, it is best to select in your drawing a positive leg position and exaggerate the action as necessary to explain the situation.

1

2

3

4

5

6

Bob Peak

*A facile designer turns his hand to capturing the spirit
of a horse. Technical effects and inventiveness are this
artist's hallmark, as superbly demonstrated here. However, he has not allowed cleverness to overpower or
detract from the mood and symbolism he has created.*

Pace

Horsemen sometimes debate the relative merits of
pacing compared to trotting. The two gaits can be
considered to be about the same speed, although the
pace probably has an edge. Trotting for the horse is
a natural gait; pacing must be acquired through
training. The pace, as already mentioned, is natural
only to the camel, giraffe, and a few other animals.

In the pace the legs on the same side of the body
move forward together. The resulting action is a
sliding, side-to-side motion rather uncomfortable to
ride. It is, however, fast and fluid in harness. As in
the trot, there are times during the stride sequence
of the pace when all four legs are off the ground at
once. Note position 3.

Slow gait and rack

The *slowgait* and *rack* of a five-gaited horse are two
variations of the pace. The former is performed
slowly and is also called *amble* or *singlefoot*. Each
foot strikes the ground separately and a definite 1—
2—3—4 beat is created when done properly. The
rack is the same gait at a faster speed and usually
performed in a high-stepping, stately, slightly
hesitant action. Both gaits are pleasant to observe,
but are generally limited to ring riding and horse
shows.

A point of interest to illustrators who may be
faced with indicating minor details: The American
Horse Show Association prescribes a five-gaited
horse have a full mane and tail, while the three-
gaited horse should have a trimmed mane and tail.

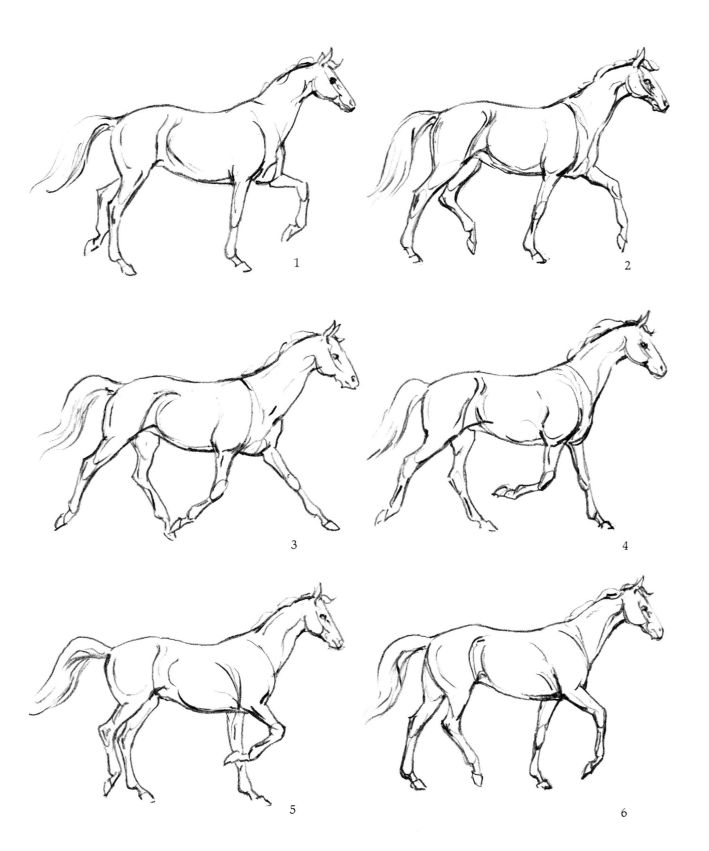

1

2

3

4

5

6

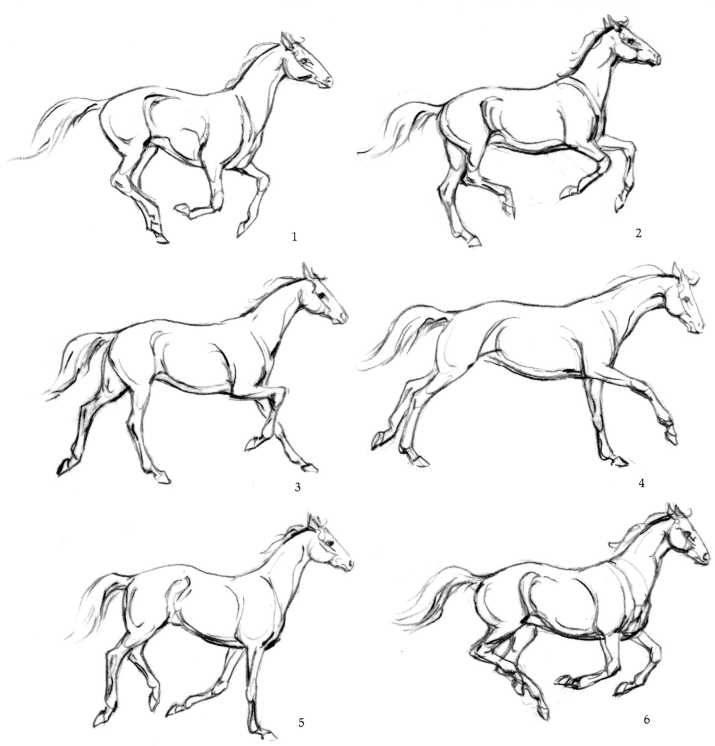

1

2

3

4

5

6

Gallop

The fastest gait of a horse is the gallop. The same leg motion is involved in a canter, lope, and run, but in the full gallop, as it is often described, maximum extension of legs is achieved. Unlike the dog that employs the rotary gallop, the horse, and many other animals use a transverse or cross gallop. As we have already seen with the cat, the cross gallop is an action where the animal's legs are alternately under the body, then they are stretched out

in a pushing and reaching action. This creates an up and down rocking motion along with rapid forward movement. As you can see in these drawings the action starts with the weight on the left rear leg. Next, the weight is carried by the right rear leg (3); then shifts to the left front, and finally to the right front. This cycle is repeated over and over as long as the gallop continues. Most of the time during the stride sequence but one leg is on the ground at a

Diagram of weight
bearing legs in gallop.

Howard Pyle

As an artist and teacher, Pyle had a great
and lasting impact on American illustration. He died in 1911, but his legacy of artistic excellence is still alive. In addition to
his many fine paintings, he was a master
decorative designer. In this pen and ink
rendering from his book, King Arthur and
His Knights, notice how simply and effectively the horse is drawn, and the gait is
easily identifiable as the slow gallop of a
large horse.

Arthur Tait *The Pursuit*

time. Depending on the speed of the animal, all
four legs are off the ground frequently for brief instances. See position 6. The faster the speed, the
longer total contact with the ground is lost.

Besides generating the greatest speed, the gallop,
particularly a slow one, is one of the more pleasant
gaits to ride. On a good horse a canter can be compared to sitting in a comfortable rocking chair. The
only riding action likely to be more enjoyable is a
trip aboard a Tennessee Walking Horse.

Impossible actions?

At one time or another you have probably seen ren-
derings of horse action similar to the ones on this
page. According to all the evidence so far presented
in this book, you should conclude that horses as
shown with all four feet extended and off the
ground, are either in the middle of a leap or the action is incorrect. Experts agree with you. However,
until about a century ago most people accepted
such action as plausible.

Unknown artist   Scribner's Monthly, July 1872

It wasn't until the year 1877 that Eadweard Muybridge, using special still cameras with wet photographic plates, put an end to one of the world's longest standing arguments: Does a running horse ever have all four feet off the ground at the same time? The inability to see such fast action gave rise to many misconceptions of animal movement.

It is understandable why artists prior to Muybridge's experiments often failed to accurately translate what they saw, or thought they saw, to their pictures. Or were they all that wrong? Read on.

Do photographs lie?

By now you are probably aware the process of learning animal action can be a rocky road. It is a confusing study. Just when you think you have it all under control you run across something that shakes all the pieces of the puzzle. My research has involved a lot of years of direct observation, including the examination of hundreds of high-speed still photographs, as well as many reels of slow-motion movies. By my estimate, about 99% of the photographic evidence substantiates the information covered so far about animals in motion. There is, however, that remaining one percent of non-conforming evidence to reckon with. Some of it is perplexing. Here are a couple of examples.

The above outline drawings were carefully and accurately traced from photographs. They are from separate pictures, both taken by photo-finish cameras at different race tracks. The actual photos are confusing, involve several horses, and are difficult to read. The tracings are shown to make the point more explicit.

If such photographs are to be believed, and I have found no evidence to discredit them, it must be concluded horses in extreme action are capable of assuming strange and unlikely leg positions. On this basis, you might decide drawing *correct* leg action is a needless and overblown concern. Not so. As an artist you should be aware using unusual animal action in your pictures may cause difficulties.

First, the percentages are against you, and if called to account, you may be hard-pressed to find support for an unusual pose. More importantly, by showing an implausible action you will be emphasizing an element of your picture of doubtful benefit to the overall effect you hope to create. The result may be akin to winning a battle, but losing the war. An action might be possible, but if it looks wrong in your picture you should avoid it as you would an epidemic of anthrax.

If you conclude from all this it is safer and surer to work only from photographic reference you are in for trouble also, unless you are content to slavishly rivet in place only what the camera records. To do so is a sure way to manufacture pictures as stiff and lifeless as cement. The spirit of the animal is what is important, and photographs seldom capture it. On the other hand, knowing something about the animal's pattern of movement will help you to interpret your reference for your own purposes. If the legs or other body actions seem unfeeling or do not work well in your composition, you are equipped with sufficient knowledge to shift and change as necessary with the assurance your revised action will be correct and believable.

The Arab

Chronologically, the Arabian is one of the oldest recognizable horses in the world. The breed's distinctive features, both of physique and temperament, can be traced back over 1000 years. Legend suggests the prophet Mohammed had much to do with the strain's stamina and spirit. (The founder of Islam lived from 570 to 632 A.D.) Despite their great contributions to science, art, philosophy and architecture, many horse people believe the Arabian pony to be the Arab world's most notable achievement.* Perhaps so, for the Arabian is a remarkable horse.

A purebred Arabian is small; seldom exceeding 15 hands, and weighs between 800 and 1000 pounds. One of his most distinctive features is a dish-shaped nose, accentuated by a bulging forehead and large, rather protruding eyes. The Arabian has one less vertebra than most breeds which gives him a short, compact body. A regal neck, strong legs, and a high-flying tail make the

*Ancient Indian legends suggests the Arabian horse originated in India about 2000 B.C.

Arab a magnificent-looking animal. But, looks are only a small part of the story.

There is a fiery spirit that shines through most Arabian horses. They are intelligient, loyal, gentle, enduring, fluid, and fast. And they have the curious capacity of passing on these fine attributes to succeeding generations. It is generally concluded there is some Arab blood in every American light horse breed. In a roundabout way the Moorish conquest of parts of Europe had much to do with this fortunate circumstance.

In the year 711 A.D., Arab conquerors, usually called Moors, occupied much of the Iberian Peninsula. One of the deciding factors in the successful invasion was their cavalry. Mounted on small, quick, agile horses and employing different riding and fighting techniques, the Arabs readily outmatched their adversaries. The Spanish, like all Europeans at the time, depended on large, sluggish horses bred to support the heavily armored warrior. With the Arab victories the era of the plodding, iron-encased European knight was nearing an end. The Moors, with thousands of horses, had come to

Spain to stay. And they did for some 700 years.

Most of the horses used by the Moors were North African Barbs—the horses of the Berbers. They are about the size of an Arabian with a round body and sometimes a Roman nose. Historians believe few purebred Arabians were involved in the Moors' invasions. The Barb, however, is part Arabian and carries some of the Arab's singular characteristics. The long Moorish domination of Spain was tough for the Spanish, but proved beneficial to the development of breeding horses. The climate was ideal and horses flourished. In time, southern Spain became world-famous as the home of fine horses. (Some three centuries after the Moorish conquest a few of the small Spanish horses with Arab blood found their way to England with the troops of William the Conqueror. The English progeny of these animals played a role in the establishment of the Thoroughbred line we know today.)

While the Arab occupation was good for horses, it was not a condition most Spaniards wished to continue. Over the centuries hostilities seldom ceased. To defeat the invaders and free their land the Spanish had to master the style of riding and fighting used by their conquerors. This they did. The final defeat and expulsion of the Moors took place at the siege of Granada. By this time Spain was considered to have the best horsemen and the best horses in the world. Some idea of the significance of this fact is evident in the Spanish title for "gentleman": *Caballero* means *horseman.*

The battle at Granada took place in 1492—the same year Columbus discovered the New World. Sailing with the explorers and the conquistadores who followed were horses. Many shiploads of Spanish horses went to the Americas. In time these animals, abandoned, or stolen by Indians, were to help re-establish the horse in the Western Hemisphere. With them went the Arab inheritance, passed on to the mustang and all the other strains we identify today as the Western horse.

Relatively few pureblood Arabians are raised in the United States. Fortunately, their enduring qualities are evident in many breeds.

Thoroughbreds

Thoroughbreds today are in the position of honor held by the Spanish horses of the 13th to 17th centuries. Racing is king and Thoroughbreds are the royalty. Let no one doubt their quality. They are big, strong, fast, and can beat all comers in a long race. In our language their name has become synonymous with such adjectives as elegant, graceful, high-spirited, stout-hearted, well-mannered, and trained. The least of the line are noble animals; the best are legend.

To be a Thoroughbred a horse must be a descendant of one of three stallions. The Thoroughbred's male lineage must go back to three horses brought to England around the end of the 17th century. One was a purebred Arabian owned by a man named Darley. The others were an Arabian (or, perhaps a Barb) imported by Lord Godolphin, and a so-called Turkish horse (probably a mixture of Barb and Arabian) belonging to a Captain Byerley.

The breeding of Thoroughbreds is a high, if inexact science. The total design is to increase or, at least, sustain the qualities that win races. This includes: long legs, light bones, flat muscle forms, big, strong lungs, and a stout heart. These qualities are not automatically reproduced by mating winners, but basically that is the pattern most breeders follow.

The modern Thoroughbred stands about 16 hands and weighs, on average, for racing, around 1000 to 1100 pounds. They usually have long, straight necks, tapered shoulders, a large girth that narrows considerably after the rib cage, high, lean hindquarters, straight legs with long, thin cannons and pasterns. In a natural standing position they tend to have their legs slightly stretched out away from the body both forward and aft.

There is no single feature about the head you can use to identify a Thoroughbred. Some have a slightly Roman nose, while others show more of their Arabian ancestry and have a modified dished-in nose line. The head often appears small in relation to the neck and forequarters. A tapered shape to the head with wide-set eyes is looked on with favor.

If ideal conformation played much of a part in judging the speed or heart of a race horse, there would be a lot of sure winners in every paddock. It doesn't work that way. Many great champions had beautiful lines—but so did many of the now forgotten horses making up the long list of "also ran." Trying to determine the indeterminable is what makes a horse race.

Horse measurement

In the distant past it was determined the height of a horse would be established by the number of "hands" he measured from the ground to the high point of the withers. The measurement was accomplished by a man placing his hand, with the fingers parallel to the ground, alongside the hoof of the foreleg, then proceeding hand over hand up the animal's side. Later it was decided an average man's hand measured 4 inches across the palm. Thus an accurate standard was established, but for reasons unknown the result is never translated into a more normal scale. Each four-inch unit is still referred to as a "hand."

In the sketch at the right you can see that the Thoroughbred stands about 16¼ hands, approximately, 65 inches (165 cm.) from the ground to the top of the shoulder, The Shetland pony stands close to 10 hands or 40 inches (102 cm.) high. Any horse, regardless of breed, under 14½ hands is classified as a pony.

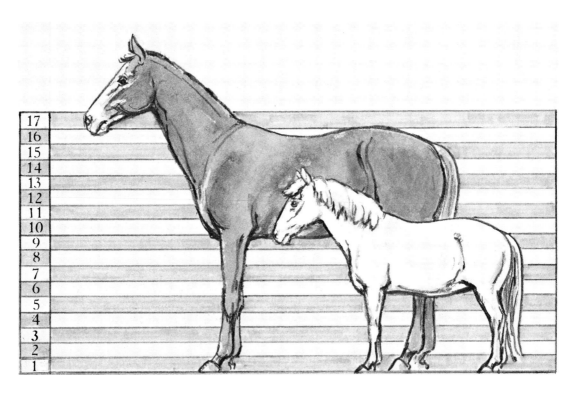

Saddle and harness horses

A good case can be made that the Standardbred harness horses, both trotters and pacers, and the American Saddle Horse should be examined separately. Certainly their functions are diverse. The Standardbred is primarily a racing horse, and stamina and speed are major considerations, requiring physical characteristics not necessarily needed in the usual ring riding saddle show horse. For an artist, however, to be aware of the differences and be able to make the adjustments is usually enough.

Purists may object, but there are in fact many things about the two classifications that are similar. They are about the same size—usually close to 15 hands—and weigh around 1000 to 1100 pounds. Also, they both had their beginnings from notable Thoroughbreds and bear certain basic resemblances. The differences in conformation and general appearance should be carefully considered if you are illustrating an animal specifically identified as a Standardbred or an American saddler.

The Standardbred is basically a working horse with an ancestry whose purpose was to pull carriages or wagons. Speed was always a factor, as backroad racing in rural America was as much a part of life as hotrod jocking is to generations in the age of the automobile. To pull a load of any kind in harness demands the animal be of stout wind and limb. This is true today even though the horse is used almost exclusively for show, with total emphasis on appearance and gait control. Standardbreds look much like Thoroughbreds, but tend to have larger ears and their heads are generally somewhat heavier and sturdier-looking in relation to their height.

The standards for the American Saddle Horse are set for horse show requirements. This translates into considerations of appearance and control. Since most of the judging is based on ring performance, qualities such as stamina and speed are no longer important. As a result, show horses are admired for straight backs, slender, graceful lines, elegance, and exaggerated but controlled (not fast) gaits.

Saddle horses are, of course, also trained for harness. Unlike their racing cousins, the Standardbred trotters and pacers that pull a two-wheeled sulky at top speed, show harness horses pull a four-wheeled, rubber-tired vehicle at a controlled speed. Stylized

1   The action is roughly established with a gesture drawing, then refined indicating as much of the form as seems essential. Notice how the flowing movement lines are emphasized. Even though these lines may be lost in the subsequent steps, the fact you have drawn them will help when you are working on the final rendering.

2   The background is toned with a middle value acrylic mixture of sienna and yellow ochre. When dry a tracing of the preliminary drawing is transferred. A light gray mixture of white, a touch of ultramarine blue and alizarin crimson is used to roughly establish the light areas.

3   Some burnt umber with a little white and yellow ochre is used to state the dark values. All of the steps so far have been done with a #7 flat bristle brush.

Acrylic painting reduced in size approximately 50%.

good looks and good manners are the essential requirements. Under heavier harness and supporting
different grooming they are called hackneys.

Other groups of horses often referred to are
hunters and jumpers. Actually they can be any kind
of a horse that shows a particular attribute for
either or both of these activities. Both sports are
usually best served by tall animals with powerful
hindquarters. Many famous jumpers have had less
than great horse show conformation. They don't
have to be pretty—all that is required is they clear
the bars or win the race.

4   *Working basically with the same two light and dark
mixtures the forms are pulled together. In this process
a #7 sable watercolor brush was used. The reflected
lights showing under the belly are unpainted areas of
the toned background. Details in the face, mane and
tail were done with a mixture of umber and ultramarine blue. No pure black or white was used. In
painting a horse one of the most important considerations is to maintain the drawing. You have to draw
just as much with your brush as you do with your
pencil or charcoal. Color is part of the problem, but
that is the same whether you are painting an animal or
a still life.*

Charles M. Russell

This renowned cowboy artist drew the western horse with a feeling and sureness that came from a lifetime of experience. He knew his subject. His line drawings such as this are, to my mind, superior to his highly prized paintings that now bring astronomical prices.

Reprinted from *Trails Plowed Under* by Charles M. Russell© 1927, with permission of the Estate of Nancy C. Russell.

The Western horse

Western is an all-embracing classification meaning practically nothing, except for the general manner in which a horse is trained. In the group can be any type of horse from a Thoroughbred to a mustang, as well as a great variety of cross-breeds. A case could be made that the mustang—the wild descendant of the European horses that escaped from the conquistadores—and the Appaloosa should carry the Western title. But, despite the diversity in type and breed, a *Western* connotes certain commendable qualities including stamina, intelligence, maneuverability and quick speed. One of the finest examples is the cow pony.

What a delight it is to watch a knowledgeable cowboy work a savvy, well-trained cutting horse. Horse and rider become one unit. The pony, with lowered head, twists and turns with amazing speed and agility. No other type of horse can put on such a performance.

The quarter horse is closely identified with the West, and Westerners have had much to do with promoting its popularity. Actually, however, quarter horse racing started and was first developed in the East. Its beginnings go back to early 17th century Virginia and Maryland, where gentlemen addicted to wagering held horse races on short sections of dirt roads running through villages and towns. Most settlements were small, and the sections of the roads suitable for a fast race were short—seldom more than a quarter-mile, whence comes the name quarter horse. In time, breeders began to develop horses especially for this short race, and English Thoroughbred racers were introduced into the lineage. With the migration westward went the interest in the frontier type race. Finally it was corraled into a special quarter-mile racetrack, and now it is a popular spectator sport.

Most Western horses, including quarter horses, average under 15 hands, and many are less than 14½ hands, making the appellation "pony" correct. They weigh from 1000 to 1200 pounds. Distinctive from the tall Thoroughbred that often stands with

The Appaloosa was bred and developed from mustang stock by the Nez Perce Indians of the Pacific Northwest. Noted for speed and endurance, they carry distinctive spotted patches of white on the rump and, at times, on the whole body. They tend to have a sparce amount of hair on the tail and pink skin on the nose. Their basic color may be brown, bay, sorrel, roan, and sometimes black or gray. In any case, the rump carries the characteristic spots.

Pintos are usually a basic white with large roan or dark patches on the back, neck, and rump. (The palomino is supposed to have an even, overall color of burnished gold, often supporting a near-white mane and tail.)

legs slightly outstretched as shown in sketch B, the typical Western quarter horse, or cow pony (A), has heavy forequarters, strong, muscled hindquarters, and he tends to stand with his legs canted under his body. The stance is such he can pivot and turn with great balance and move with explosive speed. For short distances a good quarter horse can beat all comers, even the great Thoroughbred racers, but beyond the quarter-mile post his longer-legged brother will pull ahead and win going away.

A number of horses with unusual coloring are grouped in the Western category, including pintos, palominos, and Appaloosas. Of these, only the Appaloosa should be classified as having clearly identifiable characteristics other than color or markings. Unusual colors and markings may appear in any breed.

Notice the Morgan influence in the head and legs of this soldier's mount. Members of the U.S. Cavalry since before the Civil War, Morgans were among the last to be mustered out. The horse cavalry was disbanded soon after this Army Signal Corps photograph was taken in the mid-1930s.

Frederic Remington

Morgans

By all rights, the Morgan has earned his place as a Western horse. For one thing, the Morgan was the prize mount of the U.S. Cavalry in its days of the Indian fighting. In the painting shown above Remington clearly illustrates the horse's Morgan characteristics of Roman nose, heavy neck, and strong legs. But, it would be stretching a point to label a Morgan anything but a Morgan; he is truly a universal horse.

The Morgan is one of the few breeds that can be traced directly to one stallion. His name was Justin Morgan, and he was foaled in the latter part of the 18th century in New England. Justin Morgan had that rare quality of passing on to following generations the fine characteristics for which he was noted.

Morgans are not big horses, usually running around 14 hands or a little over, and weigh about 1000 pounds. Like the Arabian, Morgans are short one vertebra. It is recorded that the original Justin was a dark bay with black legs, tail and mane; his body was round and deep; his legs rather short and heavy with muscle. Morgans today may vary somewhat, but many fit this discription quite well.

In the early days Morgans were chiefly used in harness, as they had great strength for their size. Justin Morgan is said to have possessed remarkable pulling power. Morgans also are excellent for riding, and they show well. Crossed with other breeds Morgans produce highly regarded special traits. For instance, the offspring of an Arab and a Morgan, logically called a Morab, makes a superb cow pony. The Morgan played an important role in the foundation of the Standardbred racer as well as the American Saddle Horse.

The Large . . .

Not long ago, the work horse was omnipresent in every land, and artists in the city or the country found it necessary to include these animals in their pictures if they hoped to create a convincing environment. Those days are gone, probably forever.

Once bred to carry knights in heavy armor into battle, the big horses had a status as important and as fearsome as a modern tank. But, warfare tactics changed and the slow, plodding steed had to give way to the fast, agile light cavalry. However, big horses still had important jobs to do: they hauled the world's landbound freight, plowed the fields, and performed many other tasks man was too puny to do himself. Centuries passed this way, but with the coming of the Industrial Revolution the draft horse was doomed. Power vehicles, tractors, cranes and hundreds of other machines took over all heavy jobs, and the big horse no longer had a purpose in our society.

These fine, faithful, gentle animals are fast fading from our scene. Some are still employed in circuses, and a notable few are kept around to promote a brewery, but they remain little more than a passing curiosity.

There are a number of illustrious breeds of great horses that should be remembered. Outstanding are Clydesdales, Percherons, Shires, and Belgians. The largest of them stand about 17 hands and weigh nearly a ton. What a shame not to have worthy work for them to do.

...and the small

Much variance exists in the classification of ponies. Technically, any horse under 14½ hands is a pony, but, in fact, there is a good deal of difference between a small horse and a definite pony breed.

Ponies were originally developed to work in harness. They were extensively used in mining operations in England, where they pulled carts and small wagons. They were not bred for riding. Their wide, flat backs offer a ride considerably different than that of even a small horse. Parents who acquire a pony for their children with the idea of the child learning horsemanship are likely to suffer disappointment.

For most people in the United States the word "pony" means a Shetland. They are among the most popular, and are the smallest breed. The Shetland is usually rough-coated and carries an abundant mane and tail. They stand about 10 hands tall. There is a tendency for some to be stubborn and not always gentle. Shetlands bear the name of their place of origin, the cold, inhospitable islands to the north of Scotland.

Welsh ponies are somewhat larger than Shetlands, weighing about 500 pounds, and stand around 12 hands. Their conformation is closer to that of a standard saddle horse.

Widely known because of children's stories and movies, are the Chincoteague ponies named after the Virginia island where they live. Supposedly descendants of a group of domesticated horses trapped on the small, barren island centuries ago, the Chincoteague's diminutive size is attributed to succeeding generations living on restricted diets. Most of these ponies are pintos and well-formed.

Drawing the head

Basically, the horse's head is an elongated cylinder. The eyes are placed about one-third of the length of the head down from the top. The flat part of the forehead from the top of the head to the eyes, to the end of the nose-bone forms a diamond shape. Modified conical shapes beginning just under the lower part of the diamond extend to each nostril. There is a small hollow below the eyes that defines the edge of the large cheekbones. There is also a small but noticable depression above the eyes. This becomes more evident with age. The ears are set in a circular base near the top of the head and appear to link up with the depressions above the eyes.

The heavy grazing muscles of the neck overlap and tie in with the skull above the cheeks.

The nostril section of the nose has no bone support and is quite soft. In profile, the mouth is about two-thirds of the way down from the top of the nose to the underside of the jaw.

These details are only meant as hints to help get you started. Horses vary almost as much as people, and your best drawing will come not from following general rules, but from careful observation.

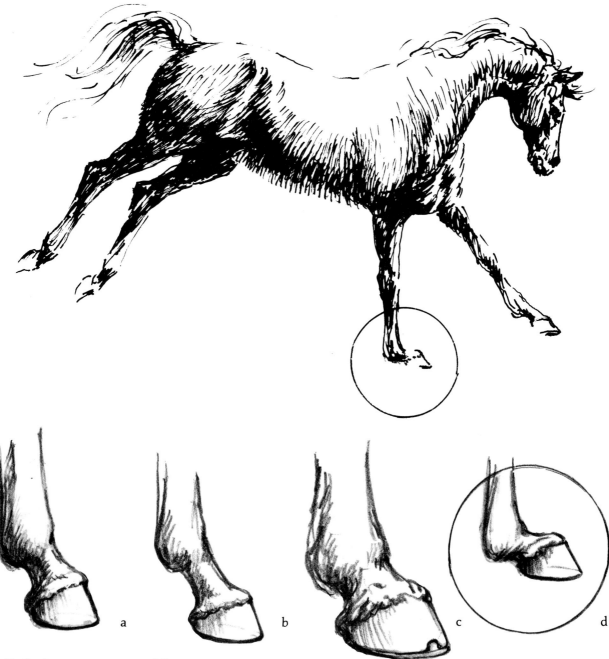

Fetlocks, pasterns, and hooves

No two horses are alike. This is evident when drawing the head, but it is no less important when dealing with other sections of the body. Consider the lower extremities of a horse. Obviously, a draft horse's hoof is going to be bigger and heavier than a pony's, but how much bigger? And what are the foot distinctions between a saddle horse and a Thoroughbred racer? An approximation of these differences is illustrated here.

Sketch A represents an average, standard saddle horse. The fetlock is strong, the pastern fairly short, and the hoof quite straight in front.

B shows the kind of slight fetlock, long pastern, and small hoof evident in many Thoroughbred race horses. The long pastern gives the extra spring needed for ground-gaining strides.

The stout fetlock, short pastern, and heavy hoof in C indicate a work horse.

Pasterns of all horses in any gait flex and bend. This becomes more exaggerated in extreme action. The longer the pastern the more it will bend, creating a springboard effect. Notice the extreme bend in D and in the pen and ink drawing. Such refinements are necessary to express an action and make an action convincing.

Alkyd demonstration

This demonstration painting is done in alkyd—a medium I had never used before. All of the information available about the product indicated it should be used just as you would oils. The only difference is a faster drying time. This proved to be true. I worked with it as with oil, using turpentine and some Copal Painting Medium. I also tried Res-N-Gel and it worked satisfactorily.

The extolled virtue of rapid drying caused me the most trouble. Within a half an hour the alkyd on the picture surface is pretty well set, and it is not possible to move the paint and blend it as you would with oil. I am told there are ways of retarding the alkyd drying time to overcome this difficulty, but to do so, it would seem, goes towards eliminating the avowed reason for using the medium, i.e., its fast drying capability. In short, the new medium does what it is supposed to do, but it takes a bit of getting used to before you can control it.

1

1   These are the idea sketches for the picture. They are quite rough and small. The purpose of the demonstration was to create a rendering of a single horse, as the compelling element is the composition. To make such a picture as interesting as possible I felt a dramatic sky would help. The dark sky suggested a light-colored horse. For interest, a galloping action seemed appropriate. This required some review of old sketches and a look at a number of high-speed black and white photographs of horses at full speed. From all of this material the rough sketch evolved.

2   When working in oil I usually tone the picture surface with a middle value turpentine wash. It seemed a good idea to follow the same procedure when using alkyd. Since a dramatic sky was planned I decided to create as much of this feeling as possible in this initial wash-in. Using a thin turpentine mixture of burnt umber with a little burnt sienna, I roughly established a background area, using a one-inch nylon brush, in much the manner you would paint in the sky of a watercolor. I hoped for a few lucky accidents and was reasonably satisfied. A few areas of this preliminary wash remain untouched in the completed picture.

2

3   Values and hues are roughly laid in using medium size and large bristle brushes. My palette consisted of violet, alizarin crimson, burnt umber, raw umber, yellow ochre, Naples yellow, pthalo blue and titanium white. Brushes used were #9 and #6 flat bristle; #7 and #5 and #3 flat sables.

Adjustments were made in the length of the horse's neck—it seemed too long—and in the legs. Also, the mane and tail were modified to keep them from being too important. I tried to work on all areas of the picture to maintain a consistent environment. This lead to several adjustments in the warm and cool relationship of the shadows and lighted area. The dark, warm sky and ground colors would reflect some warmth into shadow areas. No pure white or black was used anywhere.

4   Finished painting. The details of the legs had
been carried out to such a degree that the action of
the animal was affected, and the feeling of movement was not as strong as desired. The legs were
again modified and dust was added. Much of the
detail in the legs and hoofs was minimized by bringing all the values in this area closer together. In
turn, the background required adjustment around
the legs and feet and along the horizon. Some of the
sky value was dragged into the edges of the horse's
forms to soften them. By this stage I was thinking
of the horse as a frightened filly, and the picture
was cropped as shown to express as much as possible the compositional feeling of fear, flight and
speed.

   The reproduction is approximately one half the
size of the original.

Color studies **6**

"To paint is not to copy the object slavishly,
it is to grasp a harmony among many relationships."
Paul Cézanne (1839-1906)

C. E. Monroe, Jr.

Artists who can manipulate paint skillfully often let their facility get in the way of more important picture considerations such as spirit, movement, composition, etc. Not so with this adroit animal artist. Here the beaver and the bobcat are as nicely rendered as anyone could want, without sacrificing the power and action of the exciting illustration.

Albin Henning
This pastoral scene of a Midwest farm was originally an illustration with two standing figures near the center. The artist didn't like the effect, so he painted out the offending figures when the picture was returned after publication. In this form it makes a pleasing and appealing composition with animals supplying the interest.

◄ **C. E. Monroe, Jr.**
At the left is a grizzly pit encounter between a badger and a dog. The artist has frozen an action so fast that an observer witnessing the event would be unable to see the details so expertly rendered. It is no small accomplishment to control such embellishments without destroying the impact and feeling of the action.

119

Frank Hoffman

Hoffman, like Russell, was a real horseman, and he knew horses intimately. Few artists can match his skill in painting them. His understanding of the animal's forms and action combined with his fluid, painterly style made for exciting pictures.

Harold Von Schmidt

There is a special quality to all of Von's paintings that makes them vigorous and compelling. He has a knack of capturing significant details without letting them get in the way of the main thrust of the picture. Notice the differences and the details in the actions of the stampeding horses. Each is singular and readily isolated, yet they all hold their proper place in a powerful composition. The illustration was originally published in the Saturday Evening Post in 1948.

Fred Ludekens

An outstanding designer and art director, Ludekens had a long, successful career as an illustrator. He is particularly adept at creating striking illustrations of animals in arrested poses. This one served as a cover of True magazine.

Ignacio Zuloga
*This fine Spanish painter is noted for his interpretation of
the bullfight scene. What a restrained yet powerful edito-
rial the scarred horse and the striking composition makes
about the ancient Spanish sport and pagentry.*

123

Bernard Fuchs

An unflagging pacesetter among contemporary illustrators, Fuchs has a beautiful sense of color and feeling for the implied pictorial statement. Animals seldom dominate his pictures, but when he paints them he does so effectively. With a minimum of detail he elegantly captures the action and spirit of this scene. What a different reaction is generated here, compared to Zuloga's picture dealing with the same subject on the previous page.

Fritz Henning
The Honker
Watercolor (reproduced approximately half size)

Frederic Whitaker
This is the first rough sketch for a painting that was later developed into a prize winner. An outstanding watercolorist, Whitaker beautifully captured the feeling of the circus animals in a few, deceptively simple splotches of value and color. Why do more when so much is accomplished with so little?

Bob Kuhn

A specialist in animal art, Kuhn is an able and knowledge-
able painter. As evident here, he captures the feeling of
power and movement of the rhino in a convincing setting.
A nice touch is the interesting play of the white birds
around the monstrous, nearsighted beast. The birds not
only add variety, movement and color, they also set an
identifiable scale against which the viewer can judge the
size of the rhino.

Color sketch

This sketch is included to demonstrate at a larger scale and in color a preliminary painting stage similar to those shown on page 115. Here the medium is oil.

As you can see, the effect of underpainting and the building process is much the same as in alkyd. Except in the drying time, the two mediums are much alike. If you are interested, the best thing is to try both products and come to your own conclusion about them.

Seldom do I develop color sketches such as this. Many artists do for every painting because they feel it helps them to solve color, composition and other problems before commiting themselves to a full-size picture. This may be so, but the process also diminishes spontaneity. Working on what is thought to be a final effort is more appealing to me than painting on a known preliminary stage. True, many times the "finish" doesn't work out and is discarded to be replaced by a new "final." In this respect, I admit to doing rather more "preliminaries" than I'd like.

Cloven-footed animals

"There are no absolutes in art. No methods,
procedures or sacred cow rules that can't be
violated if done with a purpose."

Robert Fawcett (1903-1967)

By definition the term *cattle* means cows, bulls, steers and oxen. Although most of the emphasis in this section will be on cattle, the group has been enlarged to cover such animals as sheep, goats, bison, members of the deer family and others of similar ilk. Zoologists place some of these animals in separate categories, as a number of differences exist. Variations range from the type or lack of horns to the number of teeth, not to mention their wide divergence in size and appearance. Even the casual observer is aware that a goat and a buffalo don't look much alike. However, with all the obvious multiformities there are within the bisulcate fraternity sufficient similarities to form a cluster of animals useful to the artist if not the scientist. For example: all the animals listed are ruminant (cud-chewing), grazing vegetarians, living mostly on grass, grain, leaves, shoots or bark; they usually travel in herds, and they all have divided hoofs. (Other animals with split hoofs, like the giraffe and hog, have such unique physical characteristics they will be considered among the special animals in the next section.)

To further the kinship of our cloven-hoofed clan let's examine the structure and the basic behavior patterns of one of the group's most important members—the cow. Once we establish some of the characteristics of the domesticated bovine we will have a basis against which we can note the similarities and the differences of the other members.

Cattle have been around a long time and have played a vital role in man's progression towards civilization. By domesticating animals, cattle in particular, our ancient ancestors were able to move out of the caves and abandon random hunting. They learned to herd the animals and follow the feed grass. This eventually led to the discovery of how grass and grains grow. With farming came greater security from hunger, and more time to think of better ways to do things.

Cattle as we know them today probably are the descendants of two types of wild bovine that once roamed Europe, North Africa and Western Asia. One breed was large, standing about six feet at the shoulder, and had long, thin horns. Apparently they had much in common with the present day Tibetan yak. The other bovine was smaller in

length and height and had short horns. Both are classified as the genus Bos,[*] of the taurus specie.

How long ago man first domesticated these animals is not accurately known. Recent discoveries by anthropologists suggest cattle were domesticated and played a role in the economy of pre-Iron Age people living in East Africa as far back as 15,000 years ago. We have long known cattle were important in early Egyptian society, as carvings on tombs dating back to around 3000 B.C. depict oxen pulling plows. There is little likelihood such plowing was then a recent development.

Like the horse, there were no cattle in the Western Hemisphere prior to their importation from Europe towards the end of the 15th century. On his second voyage from Spain to the West Indies in 1493, Columbus carried the first European cattle to the New World. The descendants of these early immigrants eventually found their way northward and became the legendary Texas Longhorns.

For centuries cattle were employed as universal animals. They supplied milk, meat and heavy labor. It required a long time for man to learn that each function was better served by animals raised solely for a single purpose. It was not until the 1700's that the science of animal husbandry began to emerge, offering evidence controlled breeding would produce better and more useful animals.

Today the largest cattle nation is India. (The U.S. ranks second, followed closely by Brazil and Russia.) Unfortunately, as a group the Indian animals are among the poorest and most undernourished in existence. This circumstance is largely due to the special position held by cattle in the Hindu society. No less a personage than Mahatma Gandhi, the great spiritual and political leader of modern India, spoke of the cow as a "monument to pity." Although used for diary purposes and as a beast of burden, the Hindus revere the cow and think it a sacrilege to slaughter them for meat. This veneration is a far cry from the way the rest of the world thinks about cattle. Most people of most countries relate to cows only in terms of milk and beef. The artist, of course, sees them as part of the pastoral

---

[*]Scientifically, the genus Bos includes water buffalo, zebu and the American bison, besides cattle.

Here is a photograph of a 15,000-year-old carving of a bison done on a reindeer horn. Our Stone Age ancestors left many remarkable cave wall drawings and artifacts, the majority of which deal with animals and the basis of their survival—the hunt.

scene; as interesting forms in a variety of values and colors. Cattle are, and have been, so integrated with every culture that artists from cave dwellers to Picasso have recorded them.

For the animal artist, cows make fine subjects to study, draw and paint. Under the right circumstances they tend to be more docile and approachable in a natural environment than most other large animals. It can be an interesting experience to draw or paint them directly in the open pasture. As a stranger in their midst, cows are likely to be curious and nose around you and your gear a bit uncomfortably. Given a little time of calm they will usually go their way and forget all about your presence. In your wanderings about the farm be sure to stay clear of dairy bulls. They are dangerous and can be among the meanest critters in the world.

The most common dairy breeds are Holstein, Jersey, Guernsey and Ayshire. By volume the Holstein produces more milk per year than the others. A good Holstein gives in excess of 20 quarts of milk a day. The Jersey and the other breeds produce less quantity, but the butterfat ratio is higher.

Popular beef cattle are Hereford, Shorthorn, Angus, Santa Gertrudis and the Brahman. The largest of these are the Santa Gertrudis.

All breeds have distinct characteristics, markings and color. If your picture requires the illustration of a particular type cow or bull, be sure to look up reference material. Most encyclopedias are a good place to start, as they usually cover cattle thoroughly.

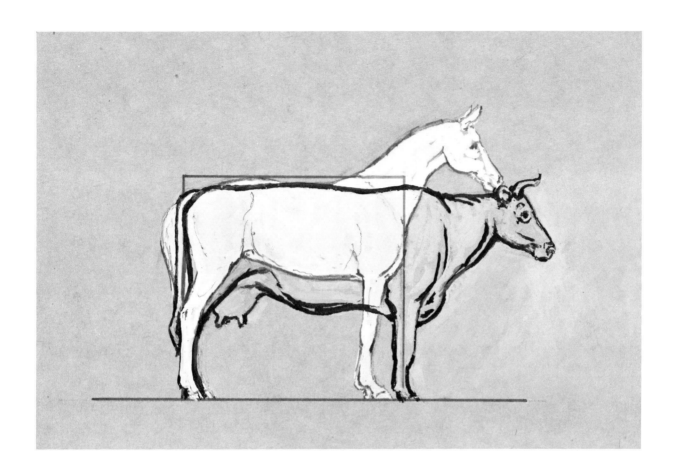

Size relationship of the horse and the cow

From a casual written description, a horse and a cow might sound rather similar. It could be said an average cow stands about 5 feet tall at the shoulders and weighs around 1400 pounds. As you know, an average horse would measure about the same height —(15 hands equals 5 feet)—but would weigh a few hundred pounds less, say, 1200 pounds. On average, they don't seem too different. That's the trouble with averages. Like the old story about the man who had one foot in a bucket of ice water and the other foot in a pail of boiling water: on average he should have been quite comfortable!

The fact is, of course, there are considerable differences between a cow and a horse. The above diagram demonstrates some of the visual variations between the two. The drawing is made as if both were simultaneously standing on the same spot.

Notice how the cow's back forms a rather straight horizontal line. Cows have much shorter, heavier necks than horses, and the cow's body is longer. The *square* rule of thumb used to relate the length of a horse's body to his legs has no value when drawing the cow. The length of the bovine's body is further emphasized by her short legs. Also, the hip angle is abrupt and the tail long and straight. Not seen on the horse are the heavy skin folds at the brisket just below the neck, not to mention the size of the udder.

In brief, the cow and the horse are vastly different. The cow is longer, heavier, and has a far more angular body than the more graceful, flowing curves so evident in the horse.

Comparing cows and sheep

Aside from the obvious size differential and surface coverings, cows and sheep have much in common. They have similar digestive systems—like all ruminants, they periodically rest from grazing and chew their cud, a process of regurgitating food from their first stomach to the mouth to chew a second time. This act is usually done while lying down, creating the misleading impression of peaceful meditation. Like cows, sheep have no incisors on their upper jaw. The biting process is accomplished by the teeth of the lower jaw holding the grass firmly against the upper jaw, then a slight jerk of the head neatly nips the stalks at the point of the bite. (Because of the shape and size of their mouths sheep can graze much closer to the ground than cattle, with the result a large herd of sheep can make subsequent cattle grazing in an area difficult. This was the reason for the famous feuds between cattlemen and sheep herders in the days of the open range.)

As you can see from the above sketch, sheep and cows have rather similar proportions. The length of their bodies in relation to the size and placement of their legs is relatively close. Although usually disguised by the heavy growth of facial wool, the basic structure of the sheep's head and the cow's is not that different. (See the shorn sheep's head on page 137.) Most cattle have horns, but they are often cut off, particularly when the animals are used for dairy purposes. Cutting the hollow horns is a painless process. Not all sheep have horns, but in some breeds the rams support superb, swirling appendages to buttress their rock-like craniums. Of course, both cows and sheep have cloven hoofs, and walk and move in a similar manner except for locomotion at maximum speed. At such times sheep often bound or leap much as do deer, rather than gallop. Sheep do not have the heavy skin fold formation at the brisket evident in cattle. As we will discuss on the next few pages, sheep and cows tend to carry their heads in a similar fashion unless they are in a position of attention. At such times a sheep will usually raise its head proportionally higher than will the cow.

Breeds and types of sheep vary considerably in size. A medium-wooled sheep such as a Hampshire suggested in the sketch may weigh around 150 pounds and will stand about 30 or so inches at the shoulder. The height will change in appearance, depending on the depth of the wool which can be 4 or 5 inches deep after a year's growth.

Peter Paul Rubens

This great Flemish painter was also a master draughtsman, as evident in this detail of drawings of cows done nearly four centuries ago. The characteristics of the cow we have already considered are amply evident in all these apparently direct observation studies.

If you find it helpful to simplify an animal to its basic forms, the near profile of Ruben's lower cow affords a good basis for such an analysis. The form sketch at the right suggests such simplification. Notice how Rubens has shown the animal in a slightly foreshortened position with the head and neck turned. This foreshortening accounts for the stubby look to the cow's body as well as the shortness of the neck.

135

This gouache sketch was made of my daughter's pet black sheep. Observing this usually friendly ewe from the time she was a baby lamb until she was attacked and killed by roaming dogs at age 10, I was surprised to discover how much sheep learn with age. In general, sheep and cattle do not rank high on the animal intelligence scale. Both rate below horses and dogs. However, with time sheep are capable of understanding more than normally expected of them. If left to their own devices sheep could live 12 to 15 years. In a domestic environment we seldom let them live more than half that time. Little wonder their competence quotient doesn't rank higher.

Sheep

Now that our society has reduced the horse to the functions of sports and pleasure, it makes for interesting speculation to ponder what animal is most essential to mankind. Discounting birds (and a case could be made for them), the three most likely candidates seem to be cattle, sheep and hogs. Each makes sizable contributions to our well-being in the way of food products. In the U.S. cattle probably lead the way, for our consumption of beef is prodigious. In addition, cattle are our chief suppliers of milk and dairy products. The hides of cattle are also extremely useful, but so is the skin of the pig. Indeed, swine are a big source of many necessary items in addition to food, ranging from gloves and footballs to bristles for paint brushes. As the story goes, everything on the pig is used but the squeal. The same could be said for most other animals we raise for slaughter.

Sheep rate a high score on two counts also. Lamb and mutton are essential sources of food throughout the world. And there is hardly a place in the world sheep do not survive and thrive. Their second contribution has been a source of wealth and comfort to civilization for thousands of years—wool. Modern chemists have created some serviceable synthetic fibers, but none have been able to match the remarkable qualities of wool. Sheep and some members of the goat family have a seemingly unbeatable patent on the formula. And each animal grows a new fleece every year!

Probably the most nude-looking creature in the world is a newly shorn sheep. For a brief time after its yearly crew cut an interested observer can study the animal's underlying form, usually disguised by the spongy, often smelly, coating of virgin wool. At such times it will be evident, as the drawing on the opposite page shows, the sheep's structure is quite similar to that of a cow, with forms and proportions not too different from a large dog.

136

Goats

Domestic goats are similar to sheep in many ways. They are about the same size, though the *average* goat weighs less, and both have body structure and conformations that are much the same. Their legs in particular are alike, being rather heavy in the upper portions with narrow, tapered lower legs. Both animals are known for their agility and sure-footedness. A goat's horns are smaller than a ram's, and they turn backward. The tail, instead of hanging down, often turns up, and some goats support a distinguished beard under the chin.

A few breeds of goat, such as the Angora, have long wool which is used to make mohair. Most other breeds are normally covered with coarse, straight hair that has little commercial value.

Domesticated goats are hardy and make fine pets, although they have a definite *goat* smell that takes a certain forbearance to tolerate. In some areas goats are used as beasts of burden, and some types are raised for their milk. The Rocky Mountain goat is a wild relative of the domesticated goat.

Although the general structure of all goats is similar, if you are faced with a problem of illustrating a particular kind, be sure to check good reference material. Many differences exist in type of coat, horns, size and shape of ears, as well as color and markings.

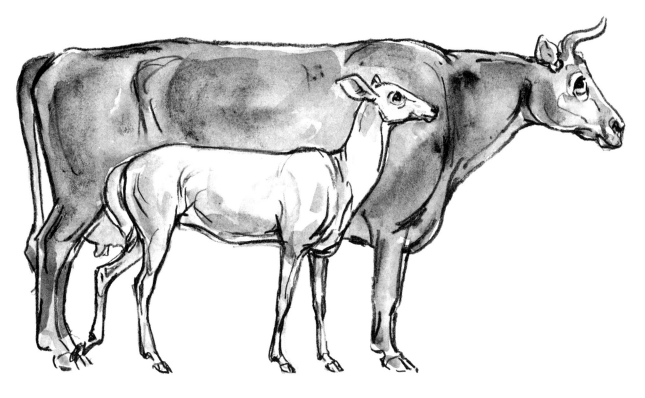

Relating cows and deer

Prior to making this sketch I tried to locate an authoritative reference establishing an approximate shoulder height for a mature Virginia white tailed deer. In checking several creditable sources I learned there are 60 varieties of deer, with a range in size from the little Malayan barking deer (when excited it barks like a dog) which stands at about 20 inches to the giant of the family, the moose, that measures some six feet at the shoulder. Between the two extremes little information about size of the more common types was discovered. It seems evident there are so many varieties naturalists are understandably reluctant to affix *average* measurements.

Just as I reached this conclusion, a movement detected out the corner of my eye directed my attention away from my book-strewn drawing table to the scene outside my studio window. There, not twenty feet away in full view, was a beautiful doe waving her unmistakable white flag. She stayed in the immediate vicinity about a half-hour, giving me time to make several sketches. (One is shown at the bottom of page 131.) Even more obliging, on leaving the small grazing area adjacent to the studio, she gently skimmed under a single strand of wire, all that is left of a long gone fence. The height of the wire gave me a positive fix on her shoulder height. She was 38 inches tall. The diagram above is based on this measurement. By estimate she weighs about 150 pounds.*

Except for their cloven hoofs, you would not consider the cow and deer as being similar, but as you can see, they have things in common once you discount their differences in size. In relative terms deer have considerably longer legs. In fact, the square rule of body and legs we applied to the horse works fairly well for the deer. However, the deer's body is long in relation to the neck, the back is straight, and there is some suggestion of the cow-like folds at the brisket. The head and horns are noticeably different. The deer has a sharper nose, larger ears, and more protruding, widely spaced eyes. Only bucks grow antlers, and they usually grow a new set every year. Unlike the horns of cattle, grown by both male and female, antlers are a solid growth. Anyone who has worked around cows realizes how fortunate it is they don't fly or have antlers.

---

*Many people are amazed so much wildlife exists in Southern Connecticut. The area is surrounded by large cities and is but 50 miles from New York. It is a population strip sometimes referred to as the Northeast megalopolis running along the coast from Boston through New York City to Washington D.C.—a crowded stretch of real estate. But many wild animals adapt and survive in the ever-decreasing woodland. Besides deer, we have many small neighbors, including rabbits, woodchucks, gray squirrels, raccoons, opossums, skunks, and foxes. We also play host to a great variety of ducks, geese, and other winged friends. Recently, two bald eagles, birds seldom seen in these parts, settled in for a winter visit along the tidal river that runs through suburban Westport! Given a chance wildlife will prosper even under restrictive conditions.

Attitude and movement comparisons

The sketches on the opposite page reinforce many of the similarities we have already discussed concerning cattle, deer and sheep. Their cloven hoofs have the same general look, but, as indicated in the circled diagram, there are definite differences in angles and proportions. The shapes of the legs are much alike, as are the barrels of the bodies and the lines of the backs.

When standing at attention deer hold their heads very erect. As wild animals their safety is always in jeopardy, and their only defense is flight from danger. Survival depends on their sense of hearing and detecting visually any unusual movement. Sheep tend to be more skittish than cattle, probably because they are more vulnerable, even in most domestic environments. Sheep are always alert to their surroundings and less casual about intruders than are cows. As a result, you often see sheep in an attentive listening, observing stance.

Cattle will, when startled or frightened, raise their heads high and assume actions that are far from docile. Illustrating a cow in such a stance is likely to establish a cartoon situation. The normally tranquil cow looks a bit ridiculous in an exercised attitude. As Von Schmidt put it, "Draw a cow with her feet raised as high as a trotter's and you will have a gay, perky-looking animal." With her head reared back and an arched tail you have a candidate for a Heinrich Kley-like caricature.

In peaceful grazing or slow-moving situations, all three types of animals carry their heads low in an easy, comfortable position. At such times, the line from the top of the neck to the back is almost straight, as illustrated in the column at the far right.

The largest and one of the most unusual of the multiform deer family is the moose. A bull with his magnificent antlers—he grows a new set every year—can weigh around 1200 pounds and is 5 to 6 feet tall at the shoulder. Their strange configurations with a bulging shoulder hump, short neck, sloping back, enormous head and ears and long, gangling legs, seem to suit the wilderness they need to survive. Once thought to be endangered by over-hunting and encroaching civilization, they are now on the increase. Protective game laws are doing their job.

If not for their undisputed link with the deer family, the moose would be considered with the special animal group we will examine in the next section.

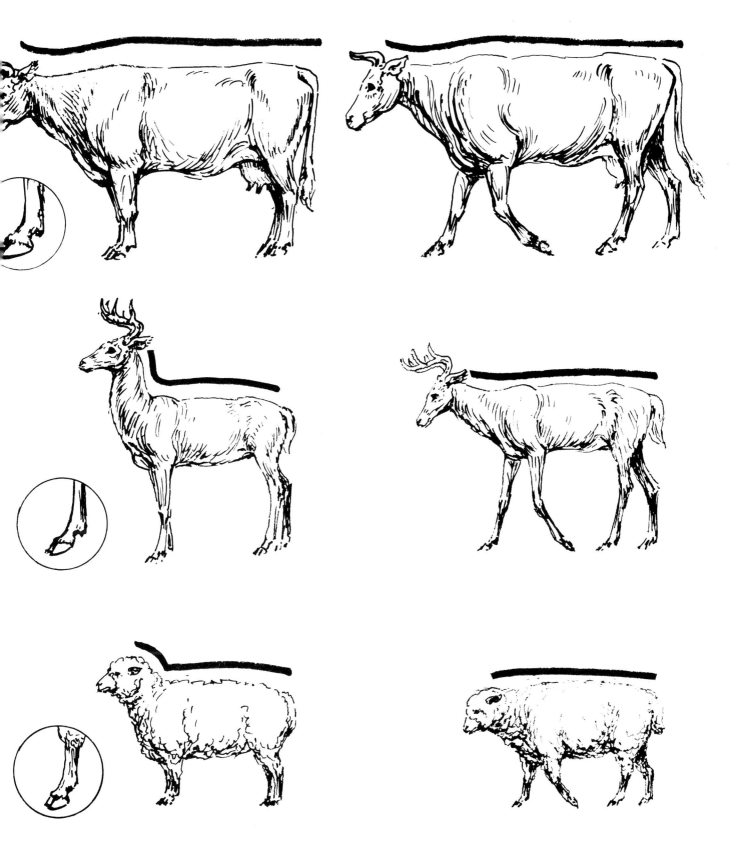

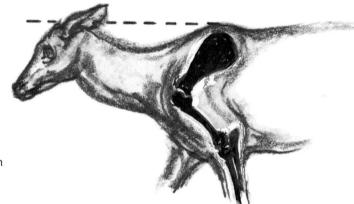

The walk

Cloven-hooved animals walk with the same pattern
of movement as other animals. The cow, however,
compared to a horse or dog, seems to lumber or
plod through the sequence. The greater bulk and
weight of cattle forces them to seek as much leg
support as possible. This is accomplished by taking
relatively short steps and lifting each leg off the
ground only as high as necessary. In a walk this results in a cow appearing to have three legs on the
ground at all times. This is not actually the case,
but if you compare the sketches of a horse walking
(shown on page 91) with the cow, it is evident the
horse lifts his legs higher and takes longer steps. In
a fast walk a cow may, for a brief instant, have two
feet off the ground at once. This happens so quickly
it is not discernible to the eye. It takes a high-speed
camera to catch such action. Visually it is more
likely to look as if all four feet are simultaneously
on the ground.

The smaller members of the deer family are noticeably lighter and more agile than cattle. They
tend to pick up their legs comparatively higher than
cows in every gait. Their walk, therefore, more
closely resembles that of the horse, dog or cat.
When walking, deer usually carry their heads low,
with the top of the skull in a straight line with the
spine, as illustrated in the above diagram.

The underlying bone structure and manner of
movement is the same for all four-footed animals.
The shoulder, hip and leg bones of the cow and
deer function the way they do as diagrammed for
the dog on page 42. Remember, the leg action starts
at the shoulder and hip, not at the elbow or knee.
Notice how the shoulder form and entire rear leg
section moves with each step in the drawings of the
walking cow.

142

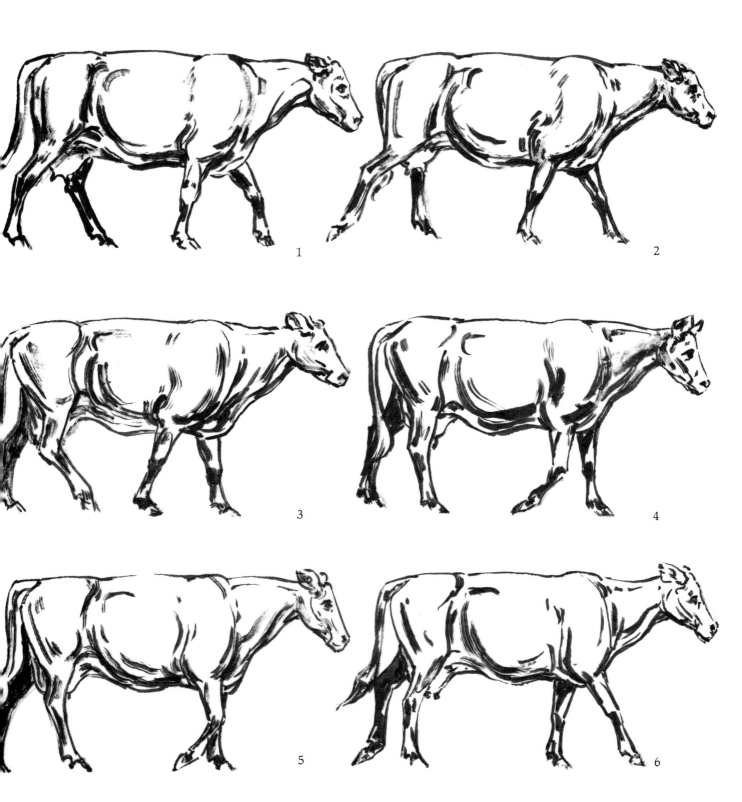

1

2

3

4

5

6

This rough brush and ink sketch of an American bison shows that the trot is the same for a buffalo as it is for his distant bovine cousins. There are other similarities between buffalo and cattle. They are somewhat close in overall size and have many of the same characteristics and habits. The shape of the head and the massive shoulder hump with its matted mantle of shaggy hair make the buffalo distinctive.

The trot

As with the walk, cattle do not lift their legs as high when trotting as do the other animals we have discussed so far. Because of this it is harder to discern positions where two of the cow's feet are off the ground at once. Most of the time it appears at least three hoofs are touching. The action occurs exactly as with other animals—the legs on opposite sides of the body move forward in more or less unison. The animal is in good balance as one supporting leg on each side of the body is bearing weight. With the cow, when the reciprocal pushing action of the legs reaches the end of its thrust, as in position 2, the forward reaching legs have either landed or are just about to land. Not often with a cow will you be able to identify, as you sometimes can with a horse or dog, that part of the trotting stride where all four feet are off the ground at once. Theoretically it happens, but to illustrate it requires too much exaggeration to be believeable. If, on the other hand, you wish to stress the feeling of extreme action this would be a way to accomplish it.

1

2

3

4

5

The ups and downs

Quiz...based on the action of the cow in this sketch, answer the following:

 a The cow is in the process of getting up.
 b The cow is in the process of lying down.
 c Either of the above.
 d None of the above.

For the correct answer, read on...

Dogs and cats usually arrive at recumbent positions by bending their hind legs first, reaching a sitting position, and then sliding down with their front legs. When getting up they reverse the procedure by first pulling the front legs under the body until a sitting stance is reached, then the hind legs lift the rear to their regular four feet on the ground, standing position. Horses go down front legs first and arise front legs first. Cows and sheep, among other animals, follow a still different procedure.

The above sketch shows how a cow first gets down with her front legs then she slides her rear legs down alongside her body. When arising, she maneuvers her hind legs into an upright position first and then pushes up with her front legs.

Why the different approach to the problem? At an early age I pondered this puzzler and concluded it had to do with the prominence of the cow's udder. Reasonable...until you consider bulls, sheep, deer and others without the cow's encumbrance follow her example. In the final analysis there is no reason; it's just the way they do it and it is not likely any of them will change.

As you know now, the correct answer to the quiz is *c*.

The gallop

If you have ever been in the vicinity of a cow or group of cows that decide to go somewhere in a hurry, you will probably recall the sound of the action as much as the visual experience. Moving all that weight generates a lot of noise. Not only is the pounding of the hoofs earth-shaking, but the cows often feel obliged to add to the melee by grunting and bellowing. There is no doubt a cattle stampede would be a memorable experience.

Although unsubtle and noisy, cows gallop with a certain amount of grace and more speed than you might expect. The stride pattern is exactly like that of a horse. It is a diagonal gallop. As illustrated in the sketches, the first weight-bearing leg is the left rear (position 1); the weight is then carried by the right rear leg (position 3); the next shift is to the front left (just after position 4 but before 5); and finally the weight is carried by the right front leg (position 5). As with the horse, there will be times during the stride when all four feet are off the ground at once (position 6).

When cows move at maximum speed there is usually a reason. Most likely they are frightened. Under such circumstances animals with large ears will usually lay them back alongside their head. A galloping cow with her ears out in harm's way is unlikely and looks unnatural.

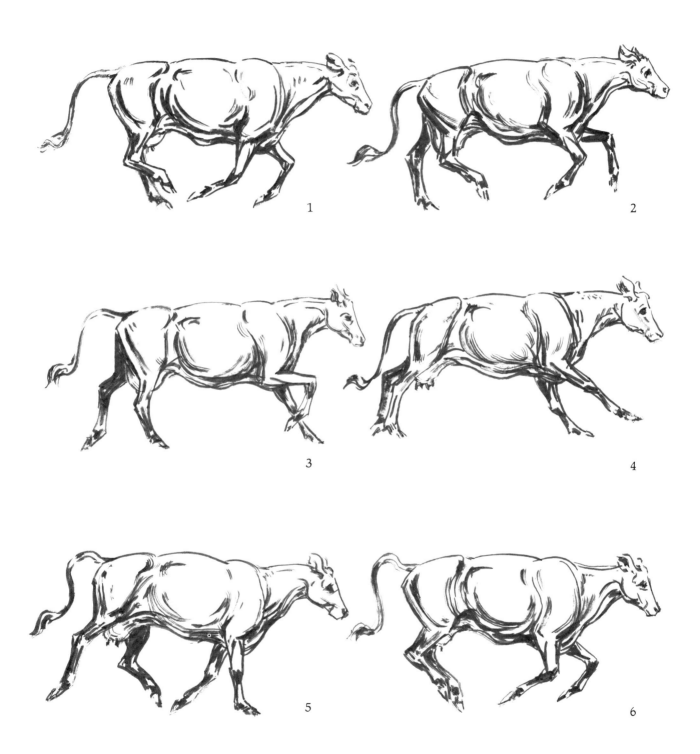

1

2

3

4

5

6

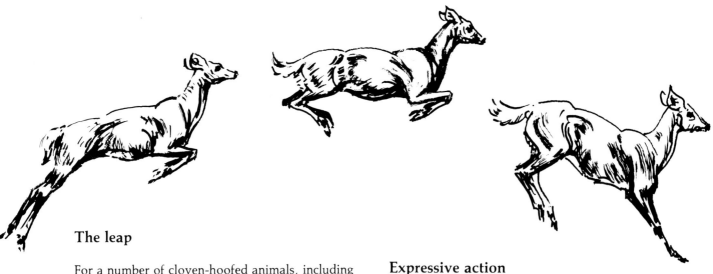

The leap

For a number of cloven-hoofed animals, including deer, sheep and antelope, the means of maximum speed is not a gallop, but the leap or bound. As with the cat (refer to page 69), the leaping action is often combined with a partial galloping sequence. Sometimes the leap or bound will start from a trot rather than a gallop.

In a leap the legs act in unison. The main thrust is given by the rear legs pushing together. The forelegs are held close to the body until they are extended far forward for landing. As the hind legs land they compress into a crouch-like position and thrust forward to repeat the cycle.

Deer and various kinds of antelope easily make leaps covering 15 to 20 feet. Domesticated sheep will cover 6 to 8 feet in a bound.

Deer do not follow the same galloping pattern as a cow or horse. Like the dog, deer employ a rotary gallop. The stride sequence is the same as that of the dog illustrated on pages 45 and 46.

Expressive action

In drawing, the suggestion of an action is often more expressive than a detailed analysis, no matter how accurately interpreted. The spirit is more important in conveying meaning than a studied rendering. The action you select to illustrate is equally vital to the final effect. As Bob Kuhn points out in his book, "A stop motion [photographic] sequence will contain intervals of pure grace and others too awkward to be of any use to the painter . . ." Step 2 in the leap action above is a case in point. It is accurate action, but awkward. Positions 1 and 3 make more descriptive and meaningful poses to suggest action.

The rough brush and ink sketch shown here captures the kind of spirit that suggests movement. It is hard, but important, not to lose this kind of feeling when translating a sketch into a more finished picture.

Heads and horns

As the classification of the animals we examine gets more expansive it becomes difficult to pin down meaningful details. There are so many types of heads among the cloven-hoof animals it is not possible to cover more than the more general categories.

If you find it helpful to use devices to get started to draw animal heads, here is one that may be used for cattle. Start by considering the frontal plane of the face as a capital I. Turn this in perspective to the desired angle for the front of the face as shown above. The ends of the top serifs of the I indicate the base of the horns; the ends of the lower serifs place the edge of the nostrils. Next, draw a diamond in the same perspective as the I with the upper point at the top of the letter. The bottom point should extend to about one-third of the distance up from the bottom. The two side points of the diamond indicate the proper placement of the corner of the eyes. Notice how the eyes are placed more to the side of the head than the other animals we have studied. This characteristic is particularly apparent in members of the deer family.

Horns are varied and unique. Good reference material is essential—even then you will encounter confusing differences. The pen sketch of the bull's head shown here has rather unusual horns. But then he was an unusual animal—a cross breed mixture of Guernsey and Brahman. He was a huge animal.

There is always a definite pattern to antlers. If you draw them you had better get them right as there are thousands of experts who know exactly how they should go. No need to have an otherwise good picture suffer for lack in proper details.

The moose antlers (below) were drawn by an unknown artist based on a photograph in *Forest and Stream*. The moose was shot in 1890. The caption reads: *Ideal 56-inch head with 34 points even.*

John Singer Sargent

Jacketing a lamb

Some years ago I illustrated a book about life on a Montana sheep ranch. The factual tale was full of details about sheep few people off the range ever learn. The process of jacketing a lamb is an example.

Ewes often have problems in giving birth. Usually sheep have a single offspring, but occasionally there are twins. Inevitably, some ewes and lambs die. For the shepherds it becomes necessary to try to match the excess lambs with mothers who have lost their offspring. The procedure is complicated because ewes can seldom nurse more than one lamb, nor will a ewe whose lamb has succumbed accept a stranger. To overcome this obstacle, the dead lamb is skinned and its fleece is fitted on a twin or orphan. So outfitted, the bereaved ewe will tolerate the stranger because her sense of identification is based on smell. After a few weeks the overcoat can be discarded, but while worn, as shown in the scratchboard drawing, the jacketed lamb makes an incongruous sight.

Different approaches

It would be hard to find two artists with more divergent attitudes about art than Sargent and Chagall, as evident in the examples shown on these pages. The childlike interpretation of the contemporary painter Chagall is deceptively direct and simple. The means by which the painting is achieved are of small concern to the artist. For him spirit and attitude are supreme.

Although skill with a brush is not uncommon among professionals, Sargent is noted among artists for his virtuosity. Adroit handling was his forte. Knowledgeable people tend to react favorably to superb craftsmanship, and Sargent surely deserves a bow in this department.

With such diversity between these artists, is there any common ground for comparing their paintings? There is.

Both started from reality, yet neither allowed himself to be limited by what he saw. Each departed from the factual scene with a purpose—subtly and slickly by Sargent, while Chagall went his way with uninhibited boldness. As a result, both paintings convey a truth and meaning not readily evident in the original source.

As said in the ancient parable: One can reach heaven by many paths.

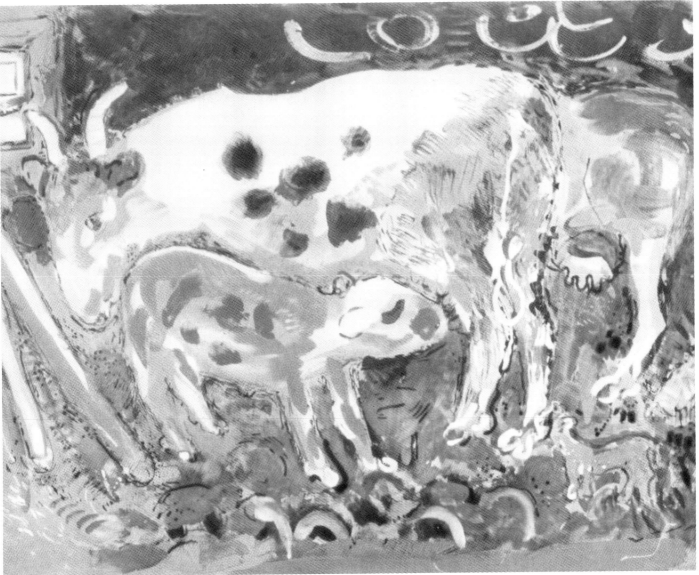

Musée d'Art Moderne, Paris

Marc Chagall
Maternity

151

Ned Jacob
A fine example of loose, direct observation sketching. Jacob does an admirable job of capturing the feeling and form of the animals with a minimum of means.

Katsushika Hokusai
This Japanese woodcut of a yak is based on a brush and ink rendering done by the artist in 1812. It is one of a series of prints on how to draw animals. The overlapping circles are used to explain the foreshortening.

The British Museum, London

Special animals 8

"The great artist has not reproduced nature,
but has expressed by his extract the most choice
sensation it has produced upon him."

Robert Henri (1865-1929)

From the artist's viewpoint we have now covered the four fundamental types of animals. All other warm-blooded, four-legged creatures are but modifications, to a greater or lesser degree, of the dog, cat, horse or cow. Remaining is a great group of familiar animals you will want to know about. Many types such as zebra, antelope, gnu, etc. will not be considered, even though we have not touched on them before. Such animals are so obviously akin to groups already covered you should not encounter difficulty in drawing them if you apply what you have learned about their cousins. A zebra, for instance, is much like a horse; and antelope and gnus are members of the deer family. Obviously, when you wish to illustrate these animals, it will require some research to learn their specific characteristics, surface markings and special features. In drawing them, however, you should not feel a stranger to their basic forms.

The animals we will examine now are those with such unique structure, proportions and characteristics that combining them with any other group would slur over their special qualities.

The point to remember when drawing any animal, no matter how wierd or wonderful, is the basic skeletal structure is the same for all. A giraffe and a cow don't look much alike, but a cursory look at their skeletons will reveal their differences (discounting surface covering) are mainly of proportion. As one of my reference books nicely puts it, a mouse's neck and a giraffe's neck are quite different in size, but both have the same number of bones: seven.

Our group of special animals will go from the largest to some that are among the smallest. Included will be the elephant, giraffe, bear, hog, rhinoceros, hippopotamus, ape, squirrel, rabbit and camel. There could be many more, particularly on the smaller size end of the scale, but it is hoped those covered will demonstrate how to approach the drawing of any type of animal, no matter how large, small or otherwise unusual.

In the sketches on the opposite page, can you identify in the giraffe forms that look something like those in a horse? And, what about the legs? See how similar they are to those of the cow or the larger members of the deer family. The fabulous neck, unusual head and spotted coat, of course, make the giraffe the truly notable animal it is.

From now on you should be able to observe and relate such form and structure similarities in any animal you wish to draw. It is a matter of applying what you already know to a new problem. You will be surprised how well and how often it will work.

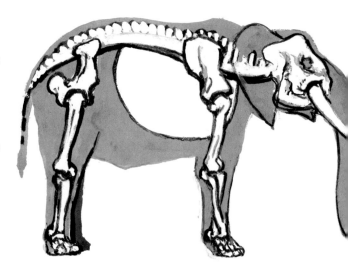

If you compare the skeletons diagrammed on pages 36 and 37 with this one of an African elephant, you will see basic similarities in structure. Aside from the head, the big differences occur in the legs. Notice the straight angle at which the elephant's upper legs are attached to the shoulder and the hip. This brings the elbow and the knee well below the barrel of the body. Also, the smaller bones in the lower extremities are radically compressed into the pad-like cushion of the feet. Four large toes are evident on the front of each foot. The fifth toe is at the back. The shape, formation and angle of the animal's bones make it difficult for the elephant to jump or spring, limiting his gait pattern.

Elephants

The largest of the land animals, elephants are extraordinary beasts. Certainly the honor of being the first among our "special" animals belongs to them. Let's consider their remarkable characteristics.

There are two distinct types of elephant, the African and the Asian. The African is larger, has enormous ears and a slightly depressed back line just behind the shoulders. The males stand as high as 11 feet at the shoulder, have tusks of ivory—grown by both male and female—that extend 6 to 8 feet in length. There are two fingerlike lumps at the tip of each tusk. A male will weigh 6 to 7 tons; a female will tip the scale somewhere between 4 and 5 tons. African elephants are inclined to be fierce, and are difficult to train.

The Asian or Indian elephants are somewhat smaller; a male weighing in around 5 tons. He stands about 9 feet high and carries 4 to 5-foot tusks, each having but one fingerlike nub at the end. (Asian females do not grow tusks.) Most of the trained elephants we see in circuses are Asian. Besides their size, they are identifiable by relatively small ears, slight upward curve or roundness to the back and a noticable depression in the forehead.

Besides size, formidable tusks and ears resembling flapping spinnakers, all giant pachyderms have several other notable characteristics, not the least of which is their trunk. This strange nose measuring some 6 feet in length is a flexible mass of muscle. It has been described as looking like a series of soggy doughnuts of graduated size laminated together. In any case, the trunk is a most useful appendage. With it the elephant smells—their most acute sense—drinks and feeds himself. It is like a huge, mushy hand that can pick up a peanut, bale of hay or a man. Used like a suction pump, it can hold over a gallon of water which they enjoy spraying over their backs.

Heavy loads are usually lifted with the tusks, which are, in effect, elongated teeth—two protruding incisors. They are capable of lifting up to a ton in weight. In such work the trunk is used to hold the load in place.

Many people believe elephants have different bone formations than other animals because of their unusual stovepipe legs. As explained with the above skeletal diagram, this is not the case. The same basic bones are there, but the end result is a compressed, singular foot. Massed at the bottom of the elephant's legs is a spongy material that acts as a cushion. And, like a fluffy cushion, it expands under weight, but when the leg is lifted the size of the pad becomes smaller. For this reason, an elephant seldom has trouble being stuck in a hole or in the mud.

Unable to negotiate any kind of a jumping action, an elephant has but one gait, a shuffling walk. The rate of speed, however, can vary considerably. At a normal pace they travel around 6 miles an hour. With the same exaggerated gait, used when under duress, they can make as much as 25 miles per hour. But, they cannot sustain this speed for long.

Sadly, unregulated hunting and greed for ivory have reduced herds in Africa and India to the point the continued existence of wild elephants is in serious doubt.

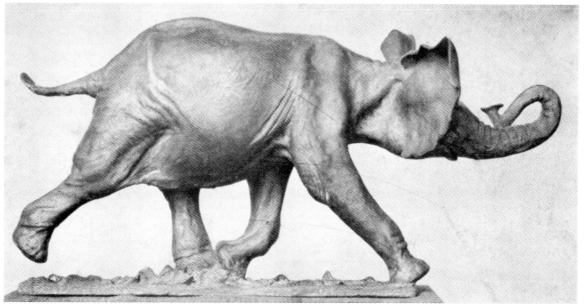

Anna Hyatt Huntington

This fine American sculptress was noted for her interpretations of animals. The form and effect of the running elephant is convincing and the action is believable, albeit a bit exaggerated. Notice how clearly the underlying bone structure and movement are apparent. The artist had a superb understanding of animals.

Herbert Morton Stoops

As an illustrator, Stoops worked for many of the big slick publications. He also did a mountain of illustrations for the pulps, using the name of Jeremy Cannon. In either category, with either name, the results were outstanding. His pulp illustrations were for stories of exotic adventures in which animals often had major roles. In this example the elephant's exaggerated size and the simple, bold use of black generates the kind of feeling you would likely have if engaged in such a battle. The drawing is simple, forceful and convincing. Note the flat underside of the elephant's trunk and the structure of the mouth and tusks.

157

Rembrandt Van Rijn
*The great Dutch Master seemed to enjoy drawing circus
animals. He made a number of direct observation sketches
such as this one in black chalk of elephants, lions and
other animals which he never saw in their natural habitat.*

Paul Branson

Creating a believable scale and establishing a feeling for size is important in any realistic illustration. How does the artist project to the viewer the fact a mouse is small or an elephant large? The best way is to relate the animal in a convincing manner to an element of a known or established size.

Here a noted animal draughtsman solves the problem by showing the Asian circus elephants in relation to an average size horse. The perspective is straight-on taken from a high eye level, as if the observer was on the raised bleacher seats looking down and across the scene.

Fred Ludekens
A nicely designed and executed 20th century cover
for True magazine.

Unknown African artist
A drawing after a rock painting from a cave in Libya
made in the Paleo-African, pastoral phase. This sophisti-
cated and remarkably well-drawn giraffe was done pos-
sibly 5000 years ago.

Giraffe

With their fantastic six foot necks some giraffes
measure nearly 19 feet from the ground to the top
of their heads—the tallest of all animals. These
unique cloven-hoofed giants are a wonder to observe anywhere, but particularly if you are lucky
enough to see them on their native East African
plains, the only area in the world they run wild.
And run they do. It is amazing how fast they can
cover the ground. I have ridden in a jeep on the
roadless game preserve in Kenya, making speeds of
about 35 miles an hour, and the herd of giraffes I
was pacing easily overtook my vehicle in a seemingly effortless gallop.

Giraffes have all the standard gaits, but like the
camel they are natural pacers as well. Harmless to
all, unless you are foolish enough to let them kick
you, a giraffe's only defense is flight. They feed on
leaves and twigs from trees, and the supply is seldom in jeopardy because they are the only ground
animals that can reach them.

There are several characteristics that endear
giraffes to almost everyone. Not the least of these is
their silence. They seldom make a sound. The giraffe's voice box is poorly formed, but zoo-keepers
claim giraffes can on occasion murmer a soft moo.
Besides the giraffe's striking neck formations, they
have beautiful markings of chestnut or brown
patches, often with a network of tawny lines. And
the heads are most distinctive. They have huge
brown eyes with long lashes; two nubby, silly-
looking horns and a strange bony lump on the forehead. The nose is sharp, with a long overhanging
upperlip. They have long tongues used for eating
that seldom disturb the silence. Giraffes are a
delight.

George L. Venable
*This delicately controlled pencil rendering is by a fine
craftsman who works as a technical illustrator for the
Smithsonian Institution. In the execution of the drawing heavy reliance on sharp focus photographs was
necessary to assure the required accuracy. The artist is
to be commended on his artistic as well as his scientific
translation of fact.*

161

Ned Jacob
In these charcoal sketches the artist expressively captures the form and typical attitudes of the friendly appearing bears. Note the flat-footed stance of the animal above, and the long nails and human-like sitting position of the one at the left.

162

Jeremy Cannon

Bears

With their comical antics, shaggy fur coats, clumsy flat-footed humanesque stance, topped by a friendly dog face, bears are universally loved—from a distance. No matter how tame or ingratiating they seem, they are always a wild, unpredictable animal. Because of their size and strength they can create much havoc with one swipe of their long-nailed, powerful paws.

Unlike the four basic animals we have studied, all of which ambulate on the anatomical equivalent of fingers and toes, bears walk with their feet flat. This is particularly noticeable in the hind legs (see diagram at right) where the heel bones rest on the ground. This longer, more secure base allows the animal to stand upright or squat on its haunches with ease.

There are a number of varieties of bears including the Kodiak, Grizzly, Polar, Brown and Black. The last mentioned is the most common North American bear. A good-sized Black weighs around 400 pounds, and some are larger.

The Kodiak, Grizzly and Alaskan bears are closely related. They are the largest carnivorous land animals. Kodiaks have been known to reach 10 feet in height and weigh as much as 1500 pounds. The Grizzly, considered by many to be one of the most dangerous animals, may weigh in at around 1000 pounds. Most of the big bears can only be found in Northern Canada and Alaska, although some Grizzlies may still roam the higher slopes in Montana and Idaho.

As everyone knows from childhood stories, bears climb trees, hibernate in cold weather and love honey. Although often seemingly sluggish in movement, they are capable of great bursts of speed. Any bear can easily overtake the speediest human sprinter. The naturalist writer, James Oliver Curwood, stated a Grizzly can run faster than a race horse for a distance up to a half mile. Bears are clumsy and charming and make great subjects to draw, but domesticated they are not. Keep your distance and be careful when you are around them.

163

Front view of front foot bones

Hogs, swine, pigs[*]

Call them what you will, but please, not in a derogatory sense. Hogs/swine are much maligned animals. Let's set the record straight and dispel some of the misrepresentations commonly associated with our snub-nosed, corkscrew-tailed friends. Hogs seldom overeat; they are not dirty; and they are smarter than many animals including the horse, sheep and cattle.

Their addiction to mud-wallowing, ridiculed by the uninformed, is a necessary part of their cooling system. Hogs have no sweat glands in their skin, and the mud helps to keep their bodies sufficiently moist so the tissue won't fry in the heat. When penned, as they often are, swine have cleaner habits than do most other animals when living under similar conditions. In addition, they are friendly when treated well, responsive, observant, and they seem to effectively communicate with each other. They also are the devil to catch if they ever get loose!

The unclean classification of pork, as canonized in a number of religions, was established because the meat can easily become contaminated. Long ago it was recognized the surest way to keep people from eating possibly poisoned food was to outlaw its consumption as part of their religious dogma. With modern refrigeration, proper preservatives, and careful cooking, the danger of trichinosis can be eliminated.

There are some 25 different breeds of hogs, each having its own special characteristics. A little research is necessary if you wish to illustrate a particular type. The physical distinctions are more pronounced than you might think. There are about as many differences between a razorback and a Yorkshire as there are between a leopard and a lion.

Hogs move with agility. They have the same gaits as most other cloven-hoofed animals. Their unique snout not only performs the functions of a nose, but also serves as a resourceful tool to root and dig food. Their canine teeth may develop into sharp tusks on the male. Careful farmers usually clip them off at an early age. Some swine grow to enormous size. At an agricultural college I once encountered a barrow (a castrated boar) that weighted over 1000 pounds. Many large adults weigh in the 600 to 800 pound range. Like rabbits, hogs have the earned reputation for reproducing rapidly. It is fortunate they do, for much of the world depends heavily on them for food. A hog is fully grown in two years. A sow may give birth to 10 or more pigs at a time, and it is usual for them to have two litters a year.

---

[*]Technically, a *pig* is a hog less than 10 weeks old.

164

Boar's head
Frans Snyders

Paulus Potter

165

Study of Boar's Head   The British Museum, London
Frans Snyders

Wild Boar   Kupferstichkabinett, Dresden
Lucas Cranach the Elder

166

Charging Rhino

Sculpture by Anna Hyatt Huntington

Rhinoceros

Scientists claim the rhino is related to the horse. This is hard to grasp, as similarities are not readily apparent. The descriptions you tongue when talking about a horse—words like long-legged, graceful, supple, high-spirited—are not the kind that flash to mind when you think about a *rhinoceros*. The name itself conjures a different set of adjectives. In fact, in Greek the name translates to "nose-horned." Hardly an equine expression.

A rhino is a giant of an animal. Only the elephant and hippo are bigger. There are several types; most have two nose horns, but some have only one. The biggest is the African white rhino that stands nearly 6 feet tall at the shoulder, is about 15 feet long, and weighs around 3 tons. Both male and female grow the nose horns which they use to upturn trees by the roots, or anything else that stands in their way. Like most mammoth mammals, they live mainly on leaves, grass and reeds.

Rhinos are unusual in all sorts of ways. They have but three toes on each foot, and each toe ends in a separate hoof. On each front foot is one rudimentary toe that is of no use. The heavy, lumpy skin of the back hangs in definite folds that look like riveted sections of armor plate. Surprisingly, rhinos can move quickly and with thundering grace at about 30 m.p.h. In fact, for short distances they can run almost as fast as their distant cousins, the horse. Usually, but not always peaceful, a rhino stays hidden most of the daylight hours and searches for food and water at night. If provoked, the animal becomes one of the meanest in existence. It is considered fortuitous by all the neighbors that the rhino is as nearsighted as Mr. McGoo. With better vision they would be a terrible adversary.

Albrecht Dürer
Rhinoceros, Woodcut
Metropolitan Museum of Art, New York, gift of Harry G. Friedman, 1959

Legend has it Dürer never saw a rhinoceros and he made this woodcut on the basis of the description of the animal which is imprinted above the drawing. As inscribed, the work was done in the year 1515.

Bones of rhinos three-toed front foot

Bob Kuhn
Here are two angles of the awesome rhino by a dedicated animal artist. Note the delicate herons, often seen as companions of the big beasts.

Hippopotamus

A hippo is a cartoonist's delight. No matter how seriously you attempt to draw the animal the result always emerges comical. Second only to the elephant in weight, the huge hippo tips the scale at around 4 tons, stands nearly 5 feet tall at the shoulder, and measures about 14 feet in length. The body is a round, shapeless kind of barrel, with heavy folds of spongy, hairless skin wrapped around the neck and shoulders like giant rolls of bread dough. This formless mass rests atop four short, stumpy legs that terminate in four nubby toes.

An excellent swimmer, a hippo is happiest in the water where his ponderous weight is given buoyancy. Their heads are so formed the ears, eyes and nostrils can remain on the surface while the rest of the body is submerged. They can swim or walk and feed on the bottom for long periods. Some hunters claim they can stay completely underwater for as long as 10 minutes. When they surface they blow like a whale.

Everything about a hippo is enormous. They can open their mouths to a spread of over three feet, displaying two giant canines that develop into long tusks. In addition, they have the usual complement of powerful grinders and rooting teeth. With these, on land or under water, they can supply themselves with great quantities of roots and grasses on which they live.

Although clumsy and awkward out of the water, the hippo is capable of traveling long distances over land. Amazingly, they can gallop at considerable speed with earth-shaking effect.

In Greek, hippopotamus means *river horse.* In fact, unlike the rhino, they are not related to the horse but are a distant cousin of the hog.

Stephanie Kieffer   Yale University Art Gallery, New Haven

Mori Sosen
Monkeys—mother and baby

Apes and monkeys

The scientific classification of *primate* includes apes, monkeys, lemurs, tarsiers, marmosets and man. Family resemblances exist in all, but there is also a world of difference between each specie. Solid research on details is essential for any type you may wish to draw or paint. Fortunately, the basic forms and structures of all do not require the kind of anatomical translation so necessary to understand the other animals we have already examined. Arms, hands, fingers, legs, toes, etc. relate directly to our own. This is one of the reasons our furry friends have such universal appeal.

Anthropoid apes, the species most like man, are of four types: gorilla, orangutan, chimpanzee and gibbon. All are tailless. The gorilla is the largest and stands nearly 6 feet tall and weighs up to 400 pounds. He has long arms and short legs. Like most apes, gorillas are covered with coarse brown, black or reddish hair, except on their faces, hands and feet.

Most, but not all, monkeys have tails and short, little wrinkled faces. (The name probably stems from the Italian word meaning *wrinkled old woman.*) Monkeys are categorized as being of the Old World or the New World. The Old Worlders tend to be more colorful, some bearing bright splashes of red, blue or yellow, in addition to the basic brown, gray or green. Those from the New World have wider, flatter noses, and have more teeth than their relatives. Some, such as the spider monkey, have tremendous strength in their long arms and legs, can leap great distances and swing through the trees making speeds of 40 miles an hour.

Gorilla
Joel Ito
*This excellent airbrush rendering was done by an artist
who specializes in technical illustration.*

considerable distances from or between tall trees. (See sketch on page 181.)

All squirrels are small, quick and lively. The largest is the fox which sometimes weighs as much as three pounds. They are also the most sluggish, and because of this and their size they are sometimes hunted for food. Under a friendly environment most squirrels become quite tame. Their sharp claws and teeth make them the world's most efficient nut crackers, and they are without peer in their ability to run up and down trees. Aloft in the spidery branches of the treetops their agility and balance is a marvel to behold.

Squirrels are fun to draw. They won't hold a pose long, but their repertoire of movement is constant, and with a little patience you'll discover they soon return to the position you want.

Squirrels

There is a time in the evolution of a work such as this when the realities of space make it apparent it will not be possible to include all the animals originally planned. Decision on which ones to leave out must be made. This brings on a Noah-like attitude—a feeling the ark can't be big enough to do the job. There are so many animals, all worthy in their way, it is not proper to leave any out. Yet, surely the ship will sink and the reader will weary if a firm hand is not taken. So it was determined: rodents and all their kin would have to fend for themselves outside the parameters of this book.

No sooner had this resolution been promulgated than my most frequent backlot companions and models put in a discreet appearance at my open studio door. Two gray squirrels proceeded to make a case for appealing my decision. As evident by the rough sketches shown here, their arguments were persuasive.

There are many kinds of squirrels common in North America and Europe. In this area of Southern New England gray squirrels are common; while to the north and west the red squirrel is more often seen. There are also ground, fox and flying squirrels. The latter have a thin membrane attached to each side of the body between the front and rear legs. With legs outstretched the membrane creates a wing-like structure, allowing the animal to glide

Rabbits

Contrary to general belief, rabbits and hares are not
the same. Scientists conclude they are of separate
animal orders. The cottontail and the Belgian
"hare", among others, are true rabbits. They tend
to have smaller ears, legs and feet than hares. Also,
they have their young in an underground burrow.
The young are born without fur and with closed
eyes. None of these conditions are normal for a
hare. To make matters more confusing—the North
American jack rabbit is in reality a *hare.*

All of this leads back to the oft-stated advice:
when you have a specific animal to illustrate it will
behoove you to do some thorough research on the
specie. There are likely to be more complexities and
variations than you first assumed.

In any case, rabbits or hares make good models
for direct observation drawing when they are tame.
Seldom will you get close to them otherwise. As
you can see, the animals on this page are definitely
rabbits, while the famed painting by Albrecht Dürer
on the following page is, of course, a hare.

Albrecht Dürer

Graphische Sammelung Albertina, Vienna

Camels

I never ran across a camel that wasn't mean, stupid and ornery. With a disposition as foul as their breath, they all seem to have a grudge against everything and everybody. Besides being unpleasant, it is doubtful even another camel would consider one beautiful. Yet, camels are, and have been for thousands of years, valuable to the economy in many arid sections of the world. The legendary "ships of the desert" survive and perform a variety of tasks in areas not suitable for other animals. The camel's ability to carry prodigious loads across inhospitable terrain, going for days without food or water, marks them unique. The physical characteristics making their remarkable endurance possible are housed in their ungainly-looking hump or humps.

The hump is a heavy, hair-coated fibrous lump of tissue and fat attached to the back. Unlike many animals that store fat on various parts of the body, camels carry their total reserve commissary in this unusual pouch. As the fat in the hump is used for energy some water is put into the system. This, however, is not the reason the animal can sustain itself so long without water. Camels are not greatly affected by increases in body temperature and therefore they sweat little. As a result but small amounts of moisture are lost through skin evaporation, and the large quantities of water the animal drinks stay with him for days. Although camels eat and drink almost anything, they will, without sufficient food or water, eventually starve or die of thirst. By that time little will be left of the hump but a hank of hair.

There are two types of camels: those having one hump, known as Dromedaries, are found mainly in North Africa, Arabia and the Middle East. The two-hump variety, called Bactrian, are native to Central Asia in the area of Mongolia and the Gobi Desert. They are heavier, hairier and are slower than their one-hump cousins. Camels are often trained for riding and racing. They are natural pacers, and racing Arabian camels have been known to cover 100 miles a day. Employed mainly as beasts of burden, camels can carry loads equal to their own weight. Some of the larger beasts weigh close to a ton and stand over six feet tall. A Bactrian stands about 8 feet at the shoulder and measures around 9 feet in length.

A pacing, shaggy-haired Bactrian. Besides thier strange hump structure, all camels have two-toed feet with wide foot pads, large pop-eyes with long eyelashes and nostrils they are able to completely seal. (The circled sketch shows the bones of the front foot.)

Demonstration in opaque watercolor

1 The action and attitude of the animal is worked out in a series of rough, quick action sketches. This is done on a tracing pad, building one sketch over another until a satisfactory pose is achieved.

2 Once the attitude is determined, the drawing is refined. The basic forms of the various parts of the animal's body are thought of but not always put down. The angle of the neck, head and hump are given special consideration. Also, the legs are carefully observed. All of these areas are distinctive to the camel, and must be right if the final rendering is to be convincing.

3 The drawing is transferred to a sheet of middle-value gray paper. Initial shadow areas are applied with a #4 flat nylon brush, using a mixture of raw sienna, burnt umber and a touch of thalo blue. Once the shadows are roughly established, a mixture of yellow ochre and white plus a touch of the first mixture is used to indicate the light areas. Immediately a bit of raw sienna was added to the mixture and some of the edges blended. Up to this point, all the painting was done with the same #4 nylon brush.

4   More white was added to the second mixture plus a little lemon yellow. This seemed too light and bright when first applied, but as it dried it became darker. Switching to a #7 sable watercolor brush, more areas were blended. Then, with a somewhat darker version of the original shadow mixture, details of the head, chest, legs and feet were drawn. (Remember, you **draw** with your brush just as much as you do with your pencil.)

Note the camel's large eyes, two-toed feet, shape of the legs, and the dark pads at the "knees" both front and back. These are rough, calloused areas caused by the way the animal kneels to achieve a lying position.

This is not meant to be a "finished" rendering. Many refinements and nuances could be added if desired. As a demonstration it may be easier to understand if left at this stage. The reproduction is about 25 percent smaller than the original.

Birds

"Art cannot be taught, any more
than life can be taught."

Howard Pyle (1853-1911)
as quoted by Harvey Dunn

According to authorities who keep track of such things, there are some 9000 species of birds in the world. Such variety exemplifies the mind-boggling variations possible within the bounds of a single anatomical structure. And that structure, although profoundly different in some respects, bears resemblance to the human and animal anatomy we have already examined. Generally it is not a profitable exercise for an artist to closely associate the human skeleton to that of the bird. Even so, it is well to remember that similarities between the two exist.

There are many remarkable physical conditions common to birds, making possible their ability to fly. A number of their bones are hollow, and their bodies contain numerous air pockets. Also, they operate a kind of self-contained air-conditioning unit; air is pumped by the lungs through the hollow bones and the air sacs. Proportionally, our feathered friends are much stronger than man and most animals.

Natural experts in aerodynamics, all birds capable of flight have a wonderful ability to utilize the wind and air currents to gain elevation and to stay aloft. They have many variations in their manner of flying, but basically they fall into two categories: those with short wings using a beating type of wing motion; and ones with larger wingspans allowing them to glide and soar more proficiently.

The largest living flying bird is the Andean condor which weighs about 35 pounds and has a wingspan of about 10 feet. (Recent fossil discoveries prove a bird called Teratorn, which became extinct about 10,000 years ago, had a wingspan of 25 feet, stood 6 feet tall and weighed around 160 pounds!) The ostrich is the largest non-flying bird. These strange creatures sometimes reach 8 feet in height and weigh around 300 pounds. At the opposite end of the scale is that amazing flying machine, the hummingbird, measuring but 3 or so inches in length. This little fellow hovers like a helicopter, flies upward, downward and *backward* in a horizontal position; is said to flap his tiny wings some 70 times a second.

Some water birds such as the albatross are capable of staying at sea almost forever. They live off the bounties of the ocean, and are able to drink sea water because of their unique nasal glands which eliminate much of the salt. These big birds, with a ten-foot or more wingspread, are a delight to behold. To sailors the albatross is a friendly, humorous sentinel of life found in isolated corners of the world few other warm-blooded creatures traverse. I have seen them only in the strong trade-winds areas running from 20 to 40 degrees South latitude. They fly with effortless ease, seldom finding it necessary to flap their wings. With but a flick of the tips of their finger feathers they maneuver magnificently in the constant 20 to 30 knot winds.

Migratory birds have an innate ability to navigate. Their homing instinct is the stuff of legend—documented facts on the subject are unbelievable. An example: A shearwater was taken from its home in Wales and released in Boston; the bird flew across the Atlantic, covering 3200 miles in a little more than 12 days! Or, consider the amazing endurance of the Arctic tern that yearly travels from the Arctic to the Antarctic and returns—a distance of 22,000 miles. Paradoxically, despite an unparalleled sense of direction and geography, as well as their remarkable behavior patterns of courtship, social order, nest building and rearing of the young, birds have relatively less capability of learning through experience than most mammals.

Birds incapable of flight include the ostrich, kiwi, emu and others. Paleognathos, as they are called, have wings that are small in relation to the size of their bodies. In most cases the wings are rather useless appendages. Penguins are flightless, but they use their wings effectively for swimming.

The speed of flight and the quick body movements when aground make accurate observation of birds difficult. Most drawings and paintings of them serve to record minute details described in frozen, stationary poses. This is an understandable but lamentable circumstance. Much of the beauty of all animals is in their action and aliveness. Too often this quality is sacrificed in favor of surface specifics. Even the renowned Audubon is accused of working too much from dead specimens, and, indeed, much of his work is lifeless. Unfortunately, without the aid of photographs *nature morte* rendering is necessary to capture the multitude of detail evident in every winged creature. However, understanding a few facts about bird forms will give you a better basis on which you can suggest flight and motion.

Flying squirrel

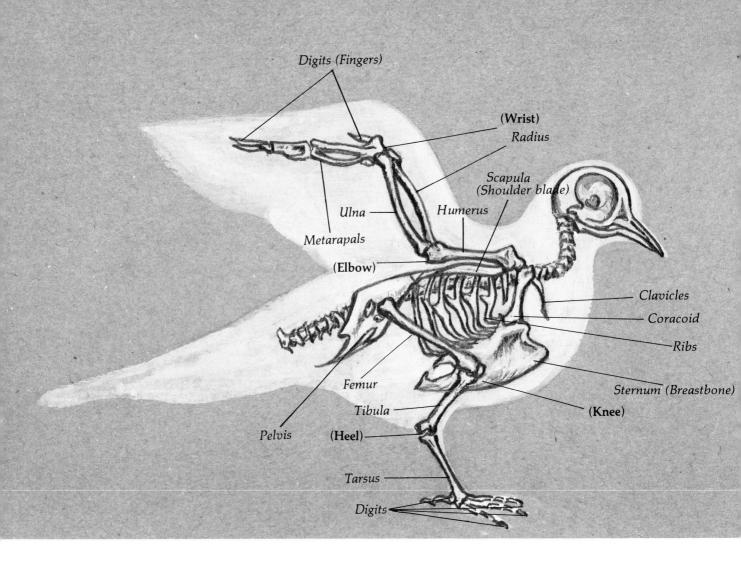

Digits (Fingers)

(Wrist)
Radius

Scapula
(Shoulder blade)

Ulna

Metarapals

Humerus

(Elbow)

Clavicles

Coracoid

Ribs

Femur

Sternum (Breastbone)

Tibula

(Knee)

Pelvis

(Heel)

Tarsus

Digits

Skeleton of the bird

Up to now an understandable relationship has been apparent when comparing human anatomy and the skeletal forms of other animals. Even the casual observer can see the main differences are of proportion. A quick glance at pages 36, 37 and 156 should confirm this fact. Such anatomical relationships are more obscure when considering birds. However, similarities exist and should not be overlooked by the artist who wishes to draw our feathered friends more acuminously.

As shown in the diagram above, the *sternum* (breastbone) is enormously developed and assumes a larger role in the framework of a bird than it plays in other animals. It acts as a keel to which are anchored the muscles and sinews necessary for flight. All of the bones are thin and strong; the longer ones, principally in the wings and legs, are hollow. There are fewer ribs to encase a proportionately smaller abdominal cavity. A bird's digestive system is less elaborate than other warm-blooded animals. In most birds undigested food is stored in the *crop* in the *gullet* (throat). Birds ingest some pebbles which lodge in the *gizzard* to aid in the grinding process. This simple but remarkable procedure serves to overcome the bird's lack of teeth. The neck of a bird is extremely flexible, with many more bones in it than other animals, making it possible for the bird to reach with his beak any part of his body. If you have a proclivity for comparisons consider this: We already know a mouse and a giraffe have the same number of bones in their necks—would you believe a hummingbird has twice as many in his neck as a giraffe? It's true.

Clavicles, non-existent except in humans and members of the ape family, are evident in birds but we call them the *wishbone*. The head, feet and claw formations are as unique to birds as are feathers.

Of particular interest is the similarity in the structure of the wing in relation to the human arm. All of the bones we are familiar with are there. Even the thumb protrusion is apparent, but the fingers are fused together.

On most birds, feathers do not grow evenly over their bodies. The number of feathers and the pattern of growth vary considerably. In addition, birds in cold climates have more feathers than those who stay in warm areas. Basically, there are three main sections of overlapping feathers making up the wing cov-

ering. Above you see the feathers as they appear when looking down on the top of the wings. The overlapping is reversed when you see the underside of the wing, as shown at the left. When in flight, the legs are usually held back against the body to reduce wind resistance. The tail acts like a rudder and elevators, and helps control the direction of flight.

Hand wing   Arm wing

Soaring or gliding birds using a slow wing beat have long arm wings; while birds with shorter arm wings require more rapid wing beats to fly. The more rapid movement of the wings, the faster the start. Many of the larger soaring birds prefer to land on cliffs, ledges or high trees so that their takeoff can be negotiated with greater ease by jumping off their perches to catch the air currents.

Shoulder   Elbow   Wrist   Hand   Fingers

These sketches show the relationship of a man's arm to a bird's wing. We are capable of closely reproducing the same action the bird uses when flapping his wings or folding them against the body. But, without the feathers, lighter bones and much more strength, we'll never make it off the ground without outside assistance. Knowing the action, however, is helpful to the artist who wants to draw birds convincingly.

183

Flight

It is an exercise of great strength for a bird to lift itself off the surface into flight. The takeoff is accomplished usually by a simultaneous running, jumping action of the legs with a rapid flapping of the wings. Large, long-legged birds can often leap sufficiently high to clear their wings from hitting the ground.

Like a swimmer reaching forward with his arms, the bird's wing bites the air forward and above his body; the stroke is then pulled down and back. The wingtips follow a figure eight pattern as they move through the air. The shape of the wing and the motion combine to create less air pressure on the top of the wings than underneath, thus creating an aerodynamic lift. Birds control the position of their wing feathers so that on the upstroke air can flow

Taking off

through without resistance, while on the down stroke the feathers are closed.

Water birds prefer to take off and land on water. The same procedure is used in either case, although each variety of bird has its own peculiar methods. Ducks appear to run on top of the water to assist the wings in pulling them aloft. Larger water birds such as the albatross try to utilize the crest of a wave to help them as they beat their great wings against the water. The albatross, among other large birds, has difficulty in taking off from hard surfaces and may injure its wings in doing so.[*]

Landing

*Some years ago I was on a freighter sailing a great circle course across the Pacific from New Zealand towards the Panama Canal. As expected, in the southern tradewinds we picked up our contigent of albatross, and for reasons unknown, one landed on the foredeck. In thrashing against the steel plating the bird hurt his wings and was unable to take off. After several abortive attempts we succeeded in capturing the terrified creature by using a tarpaulin as a net. Wrapped in the tarp we lifted him over the gunnel and let him slip into the sea. In my last view of him through binoculars from the bridge, our wounded giant was bobbing up and down on the surface like an abandoned lifeboat. I have often wondered how he fared. Surely he would have perished had we kept him aboard.

Lynn Bogue Hunt

The position of the feathers, angle of the tail and feet are necessary for the artist to understand if he wishes to correctly project a particular stage of the bird's action. A knowledgeable observer should be able to tell if the bird is taking off, in mid-flight, or landing. Each action has its own particulars.

In landing, all birds back peddle with their wings, while every surface is exposed as much as possible to serve as air brakes. The tail feathers are extended and used as flaps; the feet stretch forward to grasp the surface.

This nicely organized painting of broadbill ducks illustrates the V-shaped flight formation common to ducks, geese and a number of other types of birds. It is a marvel to watch the way each member of the flight moves at full speed with uncanny group precession. Apparently, no pre-signals are issued; each bird relies on excellent eyesight to maneuver in exact timing with his neighbor.

The V-formation effectively reduces wind resistance, allowing the group to cover greater distances at faster speeds. The lead bird of the flight takes the full force of the wind, and this position is regularly rotated. Flying in formation, Canada geese can clip along at about 50 miles per hour.

Unknown artist

Japanese woodcut published in 1740. (The calligraphy at the upper left is not the artist's name; the translation is Wild Goose in Flight.)

John Atherton
An intricate, hard pencil rendering on smooth paper by an artist who was knowledgeable and proficient in many areas of his profession.

Tan'an Chiden
15th century Japanese watercolor of a Night Heron
National Museum, Tokyo, Japan

Stevan Dohanos
Not known as an animal artist, this fine technician's rendering skill allows him to effectively interpret the surface quality of any subject he sets his hand to. Notice the careful, detailed handling of the feather pattern.

Norman Rockwell

This is a preliminary drawing for a painting that was never finished. The theme of the illustration was preparation for a 4-H fair. The artist's meticulous working procedures had carried him to a nearly completed painting when he was advised by an "expert" of a few technical discrepancies. Instead of correcting the minor

flaws, Rockwell abandoned the entire picture and started a new composition from scratch. The efficacy of such a course is debatable, but what cannot be doubted is the artist's integrity. At great expense in time and energy, he felt compelled to do the picture only in accordance with his own standards of accuracy and excellence.

Conclusion

It is hoped the faithful reader who has followed this far feels some sense of enlightenment. Drawing and painting animals can be a rewarding pursuit—it can also be bewildering. It has been my intention to approach the subject head-on, using simple, direct and understandable methods based on known and, more importantly, observed facts. Only you can determine if I have succeeded.

To a great degree, drawing and painting animals is no different than drawing or painting anything else. Be it landscape, still life, figure or animal, the artist must bring to the picture-making process an understanding of structure, form, values, color, design and rendering skills, along with sufficient information to generate the desired imagery for his own and, it is always hoped, for others' satisfaction. How do you acquire such skills and know-how? There are no easy answers. There are no set ways.

And, it is self-evident any study as demanding and illusive as art is seldom rewarded with quick attainment.

The point is, you *can* become an artist—a good animal artist—if *you* really want to. It requires a consuming interest to advance and succeed. With these ingredients you can make it. Somewhere along the way you will learn from a hundred different and varied sources all the elements you need to put it all together in your own way.

My aim has been to supply you with a touch of inspiration from a word, a procedure, a fact, a drawing or painting, to help you keep working and to try harder. *You can do it!* In art, the final effectiveness totally depends on individual effort and personal desire. My efforts will be rewarded if you find in these pages some of the answers you seek to help you on your way.

Index of artists

Works of over 60 artists supplement the author's efforts in illustrating this book. These examples demonstrate approaches to drawing and painting animals as varied and distinctive as the individuals themselves. To all, past and present, thank you. Each contribution lends these pages a dimension not otherwise possible.

Books and references

The following list is composed of published works referred to in creating this book. It is not a complete bibliography covering the whole field, nor does it include all works researched by the author over the years in the study of art and animals. The editions of books cited are those used, and are not necessarily the earliest.

A Field Guide to Birds by Roger Tory Peterson, Houghton Mifflin Company, Boston, Mass. © 1964

An Atlas of Animal Anatomy for the Artist by Fritz Schnider, Dover Publications, New York, N.Y. © 1957

Animate Creation by J. G. Wood (3 volumes), Selmar Hess, New York, N.Y. © 1885

Art and Anatomy by Heidi Lenssen, Barnes and Noble, New York, N.Y. © 1946

Animals in Motion by Eadweard Muybridge, Dover Publications, New York, N.Y. © 1957

Audubon Animals by John James Audubon, Hammond, Inc., Maplewood, N.Y. © 1967

Bannerman's Catalog of Military Goods, Bannerman, New York, N.Y. © 1927

Birds of America by John James Audubon, American Heritage Publishing Co., New York, N.Y. © 1966

Comparative Vertebrate Anatomy by Libby Henrietta Hyman, University of Chicago Press, Chicago, Ill. © 1942

Complete Book of Horses by Howard J. Lewis, Maco Corporation, New York, N.Y. © 1957

Drawing on the Right Side of the Brain by Betty Edwards, J. P. Tarcher, Inc., Los Angeles, CA © 1979

Immortal Eight by Bennard Perlman, North Light Publishing Co., Westport, Conn. © 1979

Grizmek's Animal Life Encyclopedia by Dr. H.C. Bernhard Grizmek (13 volumes), Van Nostrand Reinhold Co., New York, N.Y. © 1968

Guide to the American Museum of Natural History, Natural History Museum, New York, N.Y. © 1958

Harold Von Schmidt by Walt Reed, Northland Press, Prescott, Ariz. © 1972

How I Make a Picture by Harold Von Schmidt, The Institute of Commercial Art, Westport, Conn. © 1949

Heinrich Kley—Skizzenbuch, Leut Und Viecher and *The Sammel Album* © 1909, 1912 and 1923 respectively (Many of Kley's drawings are available in paperback editions published by Dover Publications, New York, N.Y.)

Notes from Harvey Dunn taken by George B. Wright © 1927

Letters of Great Artists by Richard Friedenthal, Random House, New York, N.Y. ©1963

On the Track of Prehistoric Man by Herbert Kuhn, Random House, New York, N.Y. © 1955

Riding by Benjamin Lewis, Garden City Publishing Co., New York, N.Y. © 1936

Sacred Paint—Ned Jacob by Sandra Dallas, Fenn Galleries Ltd., Sante Fe, N.M. © 1979

Shih Tzu by Audrey Dadds, Howell Book House, Inc., New York, N.Y. © 1974

The Animal Art of Bob Kuhn, North Light Publishing Co., Westport, Conn. © 1973

The Animal Kingdom, Volumes 1, 2 and 3, edited by Frederick Drimmer, Doubleday & Company, New York, N.Y. © 1954

The Animal Kingdom by Robert T. Orr, Macmillan Publishing Co., New York, N.Y. ©1965

The Art of Painting by Leonardo da Vinci, Philosophical Library, New York, N.Y. © 1957

The Art Spirit by Robert Henri, J. B. Lippincott, New York, N.Y. © 1951

The Horseman's Encyclopedia by Margaret Cabell Self, A.S. Barnes, New York, © 1946

The Horse of the Americas by Robert Moorman, University of Oklahoma Press, Norman, Okla. © 1949

The Natural Way to Draw by Kimon Nicolaidis, Houghton Mifflin Co., Boston, Mass. © 1941

The Vertebrate Body by Alfred Sherwood Romer, W. B. Saunders, Philadelphia, Pa. © 1971

The Works of Andreas Vesalius of Brussels by J. B. de C. M. Saunders and Charles D. O'Malley, The World Publishing Co., New York, N.Y. © 1950

Trails Plowed Under by Charles M. Russell, Doubleday, Page & Co., Garden City, N.Y. © 1927

Wild Animals of North America by Edward W. Nelson, National Geographic Society, Washington, D.C. © 1918

Wild Animals of North America, National Geographic Society, Washington, D.C. © 1960

Al Parker
This admirable artist draws and paints everything well and with style. It is a shame in his busy career he was seldom called on to illustrate animals. As the expert animal illustrator C.E. Monroe, Jr. (see page 118) observed, "Parker can do anything. Among other things, he painted the 'raccooniest' raccoon I ever saw."

Other fine art books published by North Light